I0487635

THE DYNAMICS OF HUMAN RESOURCES

A JOURNEY INTO THE NOBLE PRACTICE OF MANAGING HUMAN CAPITAL

YASSER AL SALMAN

IUNIVERSE, INC.
NEW YORK   BLOOMINGTON

The Dynamics of Human Resources
A Journey into the Noble Practice of Managing Human Capital

iUniverse books may be ordered through booksellers or by contacting:

iUniverse
1663 Liberty Drive
Bloomington, IN 47403
www.iuniverse.com
1-800-Authors (1-800-288-4677)

Because of the dynamic nature of the Internet, any Web addresses or links contained in this book may have changed since publication and may no longer be valid.

ISBN: 978-1-4401-5451-5 (sc)
ISBN: 978-1-4401-5449-2 (dj)
ISBN: 978-1-4401-5450-8 (ebk)

Library of Congress Control Number: 2009931617

Printed in the United States of America

iUniverse rev. date: 9/11/2009

INTRODUCTION

Microeconomics describes human resources (HR) as "firm-specific human capital." The modern concept of HR gained shape in the early 1900s, and it gave rise to a raging debate over equating human capital and human resources. Remember that national capital is not the same as national resources! You use your resources to improve and expand your capital. But how can you ethically relate humans to commodities? The discipline of human resources allows businesses to distinguish humans as commodities from humans as individuals with unlimited potential.

This is why I love HR:

- The growth of any company or organization is directly proportional to the integrated growth of the individual. You cannot separate them.
- Strategic human resource management is not corporate rhetoric but a human reality.
- The constant expansion, contraction, and reinvention of businesses and markets make HR dynamic.
- Constant development and compliance make HR management psychologically stimulating.
- HR gives you an opportunity to interact with such a wide range of people that even the process enables you to become a better human being.
- It should be a platform that defines and appreciates diversity without discrimination.

This book is not an academic presentation of HR theory and practices. I am sure you can find better books in the market written by HR gurus. This book is an individual account by someone who is smitten by the concept of HR. Although many worthy and well-known HR professionals have been generous enough to share their experiences with me, you will not find any dirty laundry aired in these pages. For me, the complex variables inherent in HR are exciting and inspiring, and that is what I hope to share with you throughout this book.

Apart from deciding on the staffing requirements of the company, HR involves getting the best employees and sustaining and retaining the high-performing employees.

I believe in the old saying 'go by your feelings,' and I have applied those feelings successfully from the time that I began as a trainer in a petroleum company until now when I am the HR and development executive in a leading reinsurance company in the Middle East and North Africa region. Your feelings help you identify the best way to maintain and improve service quality and productivity as you offer your employees necessary input, feedback, and guidance. You achieve your best results when your positive instincts permeate the organization around you. Your personalized touch, organizational development, performance management, training programs, talent management, and reengineering will achieve the goals of your entire organization. This is what makes HR so special.

Many business people believe that HR is a battlefield. Even I thought this when I first worked in HR, but I have realized that HR is the point at which the organizational requirements of the company converge with the interests of the company's employees—cooperation, not conflict, is the most efficient strategy to achieve operational excellence.

This requires the dedication of a thorough professional, so your HR department needs aspiring professionals who are willing to commit themselves to the success of your organization. Organization executives must make the discipline enticing for the next generation—especially in the Middle East region—to consider HR as a rewarding career.

My rewarding career in HR offered me several valuable perspectives that I will explore in this book:

- Do not adhere to lifeless management theories. Create your own methods through genuine dialogue and understanding.
- Make an effort to know your employees personally. This will make them feel valued and yield rich dividends.

- Build a corporate culture that considers every employee an indispensable part of the organization.

Throughout the book, I provide you with all necessary details for a successful HR department. I have tried to make HR appear the way it should: not preachy and monotonous but a prospect that feels good and exciting so that you, too, will say, "I love HR."

So, let us begin the journey!

Yasser Al Salman

CONTENTS

Introduction   v

1. The Discipline Known as Human Resources   1
What Does the HR Department Consist of?   1
Where Is HR Needed?   4

2. The Human Capital Expert   7
How to Hire the Best Candidates and Retain the Best
    Employees   7

3. A Noble Pedestal   13
Community Service in the Corporate World   13
The Qualities that Enable a Successful HR Leader to Foster the
    Maximum Impact   18

4. Building Trust   27
The Prime Trust-Builder between Management and
    Employees   27

5. HR—Where Credibility Rules   33
Delivering Beyond Expectations   33

6. HR Manager: The Expert Socializer   51
Training and Instructing Employees without Bruising Their
    Egos   51
Gathering First-Hand Information   67

7. HR Manager: the Great Recruiter   71
Distinguishing the Great Employee from the Good
    Employee   71
Interview Guidelines   78

8. Building the Company Image   81
Establishing and Protecting the Values of the Organization   81

9. How to Be a Lovable HR   89
Instill Your Belief in Employees and Function according to the
    Ethics of the HR Profession   89
The Policy Manual   96

10. HR and the CEO: Always a Happy Couple   99
Avoid Clashes between Policy-Makers and Policy Enforcers   99

Conclusion   107

CHAPTER 1

THE DISCIPLINE KNOWN AS HUMAN RESOURCES

WHAT DOES THE HR DEPARTMENT CONSIST OF?

William R. Tracey, in *The Human Resources Glossary*, defines human resources as, "The people that staff and operate an organization ... as contrasted with the financial and material resources of an organization. The organizational function that deals with the people...." HR, simply put, is "resources for humans" inside the work area. Its prime intent is to fulfill the executive requirements, while also representing the interests and desires of the people employed by the company. In other words, it is the nucleus that links between both concerned parties: the executive team and the employees.

The size of the company determines the sort of HR department it possesses. Smaller companies may call it a personnel department, which is handled by a personnel manager. In more complex organizations with many functions, HR is an entire department with its own executives and subfunctions.

The demarcation of who is responsible for what is very important. It is also enormously important for the smooth operation of the business. This is why HR is indispensable. Apart from providing consultation to the company's management team, HR identifies the company's core culture plans and designs the infrastructure to sustain or change the culture.

Human resource development is a product of organizational development that aims to improve organizational effectiveness by looking at the soft side—a focus on the behavioral side of the business: systems, business strategy, logistics, key performance indicators, marketing, and everything about employee activity. The method employed to achieve this is known as human resource management (HRM), which functions within an organization to recruit employees and manage and develop policies and procedures for the people working in the company. HR deals with issues correlated to people such as compensation, hiring, performance management, organizational development, safety, wellness, benefits, employee incentives, internal communication, supervision, training, and guidance.

HR is a component of the organization's functional machinery. The organization's functional machinery can as well be considered a part of the HR Department. The situation quite similar to the age-old question, 'Which came first, the chicken or the egg.'

Organizations differentiate between human resources management (HRM) and human resources development (HRD). HRM is a major management *function*, and HRD is a *profession* composed of a broad array of activities—includes career development, training, and development conforming to the organizational regulations—to build personnel structure within organizations.

The HRM *function* and HRD *profession* have undergone remarkable transformation during the past twenty to thirty years all over the world, and the Middle East is no different. Initially, large organizations depended on the personnel department to manage the paperwork involved in hiring and paying people. But now the HR department performs a major role in staffing, training, and managing people—including the people in the HR department—to perform to their utmost potential.

HR is all about strategic excellence. It is about showing a different angle of the proverbial table and is more business-oriented than the old personnel department. It also becomes necessary for the HR community to invest in educating, certifying, and mentoring junior HR professionals to ensure the function's future success.

To obtain the best mentoring, one should begin at the student level. The best HR person understands the company's business, so to meet the demands of the HR profession, a finance course, for example, could be introduced to all bachelor programs. Passionate instructors with extensive practitioner experience should work toward making HR a more exciting and engaging career choice. HR courses need to be overhauled to overcome the bad reputation HR professionals have garnered as being mere party planners or policy enforcers. HR needs to be viewed as a serious profession to prevent being outsourced. Likewise, the HR masters program should be redesigned to make HR professionals closer to business specialists than mere HR specialists. Advanced academic programs ought to focus less on traditional HR topics and more on developing human capital, HR resource planning, strategy, business statistics, and finance. Creating HR professionals who will be better equipped to have a deep strategic impact when they assume leadership positions.

HR programs need to take note of what its business leaders want from their creative and passionate advisors and develop professional certifications to meet those requirements. Certifications in change management, organizational development, process design, training and development, performance management, and career development are places to start. These certifications would evolve an HR practitioner's skill set and enable her to add more value to the organization.

THE HR DEPARTMENT FUNCTIONS ON THE FOLLOWING GROUNDS:

Employee Management
Once you have employees, learn how to manage them. Effective employee management is the most significant aspect of business administration and one of the easiest strategies for achieving operational excellence.

Management Tips
Successful management involves good leadership skills. HR should help any manager become the kind people love to follow.

Leadership Development
Develop your leadership skills. Management professionals have the opportunity to demonstrate the positive impact of their leadership skills on the organization's bottom line.

Business Ethics
Be well versed in business ethics. An HR professional is more likely to face ethics challenges in her day-to-day functioning and can assist

the organization's leaders with the ethical management of people and ethical business practices.

How to Deal with a Bad Manager

You, too, are an employee in the organization, so the least you could do is confront and change an ineffective manager. HR needs to deal with leaders who fail to trust and respect their employees or who even intimidate them.

Interpersonal Work Relationships and Communication

Improve your interpersonal relationships with your supervisor, manager, coworkers, and customers to add value to your career and your organization. An HR professional should make her communication encouraging, compassionate, lucid, and empowering.

Employee Performance Management

This critical function deals with employee performance improvement, development, training, cross-training for challenging assignments as well as personal and career growth, 360-degree feedback, and ongoing performance feedback. Performance appraisals or annual reviews are also necessary.

Daily Performance Management

This involves helping managers and employees set goals, make their expectations clear, and provide effective and valuable feedback—all of which contributes to an effective performance management system.

Performance Goal-Setting

Identifying the right goals and the right metrics for measuring employee achievement is the foundation for business success since it enables the organization to achieve its resolutions and forward progress according to an individual employee's development plan and the organization's strategic objectives.

WHERE IS HR NEEDED?

Whenever executive management wants or needs to systematize and enforce policies, it turns to HR. With organizations becoming more adaptable, resilient, and customer-centered, HR has gained a strategic position as an employee sponsor and mentor in identifying and executing desirable changes in organizational culture. HR fulfills these responsibilities:

- recruiting;
- hiring;

- training;
- coaching;
- performance management;
- organizational development;
- leadership development;
- internal communication;
- employee relations;
- policy recommendation;
- compensation, including salary, benefits, and incentives;
- team-building; and
- social activities.

The ability of HR managers to contribute has resulted in HR's position as a strategic partner of the organization. They are required to play a part in the accomplishment of the organization's objectives.

Companies expect HR managers to hold a pivotal role as a strategic employee sponsor and advocate. Their expertise lies in creating a workforce that is competent, concerned, and committed to the company's objectives. The HR professional must establish an organizational culture that promotes effective methods of goal-setting, communication, and empowerment.

HR professionals should foster positive and productive changes consistently and repeatedly. The HR leader who is knowledgeable about the company culture and is able to execute winning tactics according to the needs of the company is highly valued.

A successful HR leader forms a meaningful connection between employees and management, encouraging employee satisfaction (diminishing employee discontent) and fostering needed change (decreasing resistance to change). This is how the HR professional becomes invaluable and indispensable for the organization, which continuously assesses the effectiveness of the HR function.

CHAPTER 2

THE HUMAN CAPITAL EXPERT

HOW TO HIRE THE BEST CANDIDATES AND RETAIN THE BEST EMPLOYEES

The vast majority of HR activities deal with the development of an organization's human capital through routine recruitment of high-quality candidates to fill vacancies and things like interviews, reference checks, hiring, compensation, and appointment letters.

A worthy HR professional is expected to adopt a talent management strategy that understands the actual requirements of each particular job along with the education, experience, and wisdom of applicants who may fill those jobs. These are necessities to better develop and manage human capital in the organization. HR needs to take a strategic approach to cultivate this most valuable asset. This approach, in turn, will open gateways to improved performance and future development of the organization. A targeted employee performance coaching plan should be established to get a substantial and constant return on the organization's training investments. The plan will identify the developmental requirements and goals of the team members and hold them accountable for their performance.

A human capital expert actually changes the focus from simply managing talent to actually leading and developing talent. Today, the talent management industry strongly emphasizes attracting and recruiting talent with a lesser emphasis on long-term talent development. Leadership—the key to success for long-term talent development—ought to be closely allied to the organization's overall strategic aspirations. HR experts must encourage individuals to meet their true potential. They should also put effective succession planning into practice to develop a pipeline of qualified leaders who will meet the future needs of the organization. All that is required is an innovative approach that will empower individuals to take control.

A human capital expert builds a winning organization to achieve:

- a clear vision and a mission that makes sense to everyone on the organization chart.
- profit and customer loyalty.
- employee satisfaction.
- employee and customer loyalty.
- retention of its top performers.
- leadership in its chosen market or markets.

It is important to standardize the hiring process. Mere dependence on conversational skills to choose between candidates is not enough. At the basic level, the hiring process should consist of criteria-based screening of an adequate number of candidates, background checks, standardized assessments, and structured interviews. The steps for recruiting and selecting qualified employees can be simple.

1. A department head informs the HR manager of an opening in her department.
2. The HR manager formulates a job description for publication, either internally or publicly.
3. HR fields the responses to the job announcement to separate the qualified from the unqualified applicants.
4. After this, the interview process is coordinated with the few whose resumes meet the qualifications and impress HR.
5. The HR manager schedules interviews with the hiring managers and the potential candidates.

All the while, HR oversees skill development of the company's workforce. After the hiring process concludes, the HR department acts as an in-house training center for the new recruits. Depending on the requirements, it conducts training programs either on-site or off-site and with internal resources or vendors with particular expertise.

HIRING TOP TALENT IS DONE BY THE HUMAN CAPITAL EXPERT AND CONSISTS OF:

- ***Recruiting the Right People for the Organization.*** In his book, *Good to Great,* Jim Collins talks about the importance of having the right talent on the organizational bus. Hire individuals who fit your culture and work environment. The applicant's desire to accomplish something in the position dramatically increases the probability of that employee being content with her effort, and therefore, the likelihood that she will remain with the organization for an extended period of time. This can be rephrased as, "Hire individuals who perfectly merge with the demands of the company."

- ***Communicate Continuously.*** Emphasize workplace communication, but do not make it seem cliché. Constant, credible, and meaningful communication is vital to retain employees. Ensure that employees are aware of their responsibilities and accountabilities. Communicate every required company strategy or plan to all employees so everyone is in the loop.

- ***Make an Effort to Include Employees in Decision-Making.*** Include them in the process, particularly when those decisions will directly affect the individual's department or work area. You can create a culture of employee involvement that may produce new ideas and innovations that would not have been considered by management.

- ***Encourage Employees to Contribute to the Knowledge Pool.*** When individuals share their information, it retains the maximum information for the organization. Organize conferences and training workshops to let everyone know she is a valuable member of the organization. It will be just as advantageous for the employees as for the managers and leaders.

- ***Enhance the Feedback Loop.*** Most employees appreciate regular feedback about their performance. Expand that process beyond the annual performance review and make it part of your organization's day-to-day routine. Feedback does not need to be ceremonial. Simply stop by an employee's desk and compliment her work or tell her about a current project. Such continuous communication can tremendously boost her morale and help retention.

- ***Suggest a Competitive and Appropriate Compensation Package.*** The organization ought to pay fairly for the work of an employee. Research what other organizations pay for a similar job and set your compensation accordingly.
- ***Maintain Equilibrium in Work and Personal Life.*** Family is of utmost importance for everyone, and money cannot compensate for family strain. Emphasize the significance of a work-life balance. Permit a worker who meets expectations to take an extended lunch or excuse her to watch her son's football game. You are likely to be rewarded with dependability and extended service to the organization.
- ***Plan for Employee Growth and Development.*** Provide opportunities for employees to attain new skills and expertise that will be useful to them and to the organization. Consider transferring an employee to another department if she seems bored or burnt out in her current placement. Such a transfer will be understood as an act of welcome attention on your part.
- ***Recognize Hard Work and Make Employees Feel Valued.*** This is arguably the greatest factor in employee retention. Employees from every level of the organization want their work to be valued and acknowledged. You can decide whether the acknowledgment can be simple or elaborate, but a quick thanks or a congratulatory e-mail can improve an employee's confidence.
- ***Clearly Articulate What Is Expected from Employees.*** Employees can get very discouraged and frustrated if they do not have a clear understanding of expectation. It promotes undue fear and anxiety and may even trigger an angry outburst when an employee receives a negative performance evaluation.
- ***Improve Leadership, Management, and Mentorship.*** Studies repeatedly demonstrate that employees leave bosses not jobs. HR plays a significant role in employee success by counseling and coaching leaders to be respectful, considerate, and affable. They should provide clear performance expectations, live up to promises, and create an atmosphere in which employees can thrive.
- ***Provide Just and Impartial Treatment to All Employees.*** Do not allow animosity and resentment to develop. Do not promote favoritism. Both of these can be lethal for workers' motivation and performance, so avoid them at all costs.

- ***Become a Supportive Servant Leader.*** Servant leaders are not *soft* leaders. They establish accountability for themselves and their groups by creating an encouraging work environment. They always try to:
  - boost and sustain others;
  - have faith that people want to achieve something;
  - focus on empowerment rather than their own power;
  - share information and incorporate others into it;
  - concentrate on accountability rather than on placing blame;
  - proactively search for opportunities to improve colleagues;
  - eradicate barriers to employees' success;
  - treat every individual in the organization like a valued patron;
  - keep the image of satisfied customers in focus throughout the organization; and
  - develop and implement an inspiring work atmosphere.

Clear management jargon out of the atmosphere and promote an easy, healthy work environment. Here are a few examples of how dissatisfied or suspicious employees may interpret cliché phrases in an unhealthy organization:

- Stating that the employee must be deadline oriented before telling her about her responsibilities means, 'You'll be six months behind schedule the moment you start your work.'
- Before advising the employee about the work culture and what is required of her, saying "We have a casual work atmosphere" might be interpreted as, "We do not pay enough to dress professionally."
- When you say that some overtime is required, do not mean every evening and every weekend.
- Do not be so strict as to say that there cannot be a sick day by stating that 'If you are well enough to visit the doctor, you must be well enough to arrive for work.'

Chapter 3

A Noble Pedestal

Community Service in the Corporate World

HR builds its own community system, consisting of the current, former, and future employees. The company banks on HR to promote a certain system, culture, and mode of functioning that will help a strong community sentiment to flourish. Together with management, HR builds a leadership to cultivate stability, hope, growth, and development for all of the community's members and constituents. The environment should be encouraging enough to provide natural motivation, which will, in turn, create a superior work culture and aid employee retention.

This healthy and positive interrelationship will nurture the dream of success through employees' ready willingness to perform to the fullest potential and even sacrifice for better company prospects. No wonder, HR is hailed as a community service in the corporate world.

A rough overview of what HR service entails in the corporate world is given below:

- The company includes the executive and nonexecutive employees. HR is responsible for providing all of them with the required and relevant information for their respective positions. HR is also supposed to provide advisory and consultative services.
- HR has a clearly articulated policy or guideline for dealing with all routine matters and setting expectations for responding to unanticipated situations. It is the HR manager's duty to ensure that

employees understand and comply with the guidelines. She needs to promote progress, accomplishment, and application of effective business strategies in the context of HR policies and procedures.

- HR is expected to act as a facilitator for effective recruitment. HR is also responsible for the successful employment and efficient deployment of departmental employees.

- The innovative HR manager must always generate ideas. She is required to continuously provide suggestions for developing and upgrading the existing recruitment policies for the company. She should also be able to recommend meaningful, necessary changes according to requirements.

- HR must work in tandem with the hiring manager to develop accurate job descriptions. The personnel requisitions should be thoroughly reviewed.

- The HR manager should be able to identify the proper recruitment sources competently. A successful source will provide her with applicants who are eligible and qualified. She can use routine and nonroutine methods to aid her. She should be able to establish good professional relationships with the relevant colleges and universities. She should have access to the best job fairs and professional organizations.

- The HR manager must have excellent public relations skills. The department should be able to create and promote good advertising strategies to achieve successful recruitment. The respective medium of communication must be reasonably decided on. Efficacy lies in targeting only appropriately qualified applicants.

- Proper plans should be coordinated between the HR manager and the hiring manager to screen and review resumes and applications. The arrangement and conduct of the interviews must also be well organized. Selection and salary issues should also be sorted out between them.

- The HR manager must perform reference checks and initiate background investigations. She is responsible for preparing offer letters and verbal job offers and issuing other necessary forms.

- A skilled HR manager should anticipate, identify, and resolve employee issues. This may encompass employment, employee relations, compensation, benefits, and training and development, to name just a few. Not only that, she must investigate and resolve any complaints or charges that might arise.

- Recruitment procedures must conform to the government's laws, and the duty of the HR leader is to ensure compliance even across international boundaries.
- The HR professional is expected to consult regularly with management regarding matters of employee relations, different job classifications, and employee morale. It is the responsibility of the HR manager to prevent problems from cropping up in these and other areas and, if a problem occurs despite anticipation and preparation, to solve them immediately.

In short, the fundamental principle of HR service is to devise and implement an HR strategy that will help the company to attract, develop, and retain a diverse, occupied, industrious, and brilliant workforce.

HR plays a pivotal role in the company's growth and structure. The HR manager becomes the guiding force and, thus, the leader in shaping the company. A successful HR manager leads and enables the organization and its employees to achieve amazing results.

The following four famous quotes give an overview of the all-encompassing role of a great leadership.

- Peter F. Drucker: "Leadership is not magnetic personality—that can just as well be a glib tongue. It is not 'making friends and influencing people'—that is flattery. Leadership is lifting a person's vision to higher sights, the raising of a person's performance to a higher standard, the building of a personality beyond its normal limitations."
- John Maxwell: "The first step to leadership is servanthood."
- Warren Bennis: "Leadership is the capacity to create a compelling vision and translate it into action and sustain it. Successful leaders have a vision that other people believe in and treat as their own."

The impact of HR services and functions is directly related to corporate social responsibility (CSR) and social justice. That particular aspect of HR's function reveals the impact it has on the society at large. The challenges faced by the company are, to a large extent, buffered by CSR. What is required is to broaden the horizon, support local initiatives, make decisions that are not for profit and perform small charities within the organization. A significant difference in the corporate world is achieved with these goals in mind.

The impact has its origination when HR focuses on something that helps the company's sustainable competitive position by not merely engaging employees in that act but also acting as an active and responsible source of meaning and motivation. HR needs to take the lead in providing the opportunity by aligning management and HR processes to achieve an effective result. The impact is manifested in a healthy, ethical, sustainable, and motivated workforce.

Statistically, corporations today control about 25 percent of the world's assets. Therefore, it is the ethical responsibility of the HR leader to give back to the society. Most companies tend to contribute to the society through not for profit trusts and foundations by means of well-defined corporate citizenship initiatives.

But this should not be some run-of-the-mill charity work. HR needs to redefine the act of giving back. HR is required to encourage social entrepreneurship within the society by investing the same degree of focus and energy that they normally invest in making the business profitable.

With the awakening of the conscience, HR needs to take the initiative to reform. This is the era of youth, with most of the workforce within the age bracket between thirty and forty-five years of age, and the power to initiate change lies within the very system itself. The HR department needs to do its bit through in-house governance, organizational policy-making, and contributions to the improvement of the civic mentality.

You can find many HR professionals with ground-breaking ideas, but they lack the means and resources to execute them. So when HR leaders become the agents of change, the maximum positive difference is made possible.

The challenge before the HR executive is quite formidable. She must ensure social responsibility through positive business results. The dilemma lies in whether the HR professional should lead by example or by policy.

Let us look at the impact on recruitment.

A non-biased and impartial recruitment provides a suitable and productive candidate. A candidate is not naïve; she is aware of the reasons why she is selected. So, when she becomes conscious that she is an impartial choice, she becomes all the more responsive to the expectations that the company has for her. She becomes sensitive about her work and focuses on the company's positive prospects.

The HR leader, in this example, fosters a sense of impartial social behavior. Her decision is free from any sort of discrimination on grounds of caste, religion, gender, or skin color. She promotes a universal work culture.

Recruitment being the first step toward introducing the employee into the corporate forum, its implications are critical. Promoting the work culture and ethics in the specific environment of the company come next. An employee who is a product of an unbiased recruitment can easily relate to the company's nondiscrimination requirements since her notion of self-development is naturally aligned with that of the company. Her personal sense of profit and sustainability is parallel to that of the company. Her ethical business conduct works toward promoting that same work culture for future recruits.

Effective employee retention can also be promoted by an unprejudiced HR system. The social impact is enhanced by personalized interactions. This setup makes employees feel comfortable, and HR can then discuss any problems regarding work performance with ease. A thoughtful and acceptable solution can also originate in an engaging discussion. This personalized rapport has been proven to dramatically increase the productivity level of employees. Further, an undoubted loyalty to the company is gained.

The process of encouraging skill development is aimed at making the employee more capable and productive. But something more is achieved in the process. New or improved skills undoubtedly benefit the employee and increase her self-confidence. Knowledge can be purely technical, but when infused with a sense of morality and ethics, can prove the most effective combination to foster self-improvement.

The major achievement of this is the team-building aspect. The HR system helps employees learn the dynamics of social responsibility. As they say, "charity begins at home." Similarly, the sense of collective responsibility instilled in employees goes a long way toward enabling them to understand their social responsibilities and fulfill their expected roles.

In addition to this, there is also the aspect of independence, which is a natural outcome of a sense of responsibility. When an individual begins to be responsible and happy in her work atmosphere, then quite naturally, her productivity increases, and she becomes a much happier person at home. A happy person in the family is a happy social individual too. This theory is a bit debatable, though.

Actually, the process may run the other direction, too. But, whatever the direction, society stands as the beneficiary.

THE QUALITIES THAT ENABLE A SUCCESSFUL HR LEADER TO FOSTER THE MAXIMUM IMPACT

She Must Be Self-Confident and Optimistic

The HR professional is expected to be a thorough leader. A leader's self-confidence is of prime importance, because the confidence of the HR leader permeates the workforce. Even a hopelessly laid-back cabin crew will jump into action because of the supreme self-confidence of the captain of the ship. The HR professional always needs to be optimistically upbeat.

She cannot afford to be weighed down by challenges or negative developments. A positive futuristic vision will enable her to find effective solutions to the existing problems and help her face challenges head-on. In the concept of teamwork, which is the functional style of all corporate industries, confidence and optimism is contagious to a great extent, especially when from the team leader.

She Must Be Able to Take Calculated Risks

Being confident and optimistic does not mean that a person behaves rashly. An HR professional is accountable for the company's development. There are bound to be challenges and risks in the course of life, and this is, of course, true for HR functions as well. For an effective solution, it may so happen that she needs to undertake a certain amount of risk.

A successful HR professional must be able to make a reasonable judgment regarding whether the amount of risk that she is undertaking is worth the anticipated result. Her mere confidence about the outcome is not a buffer against the probability of a negative result, so any risk needs to be a calculated one.

She Must Respond Positively to Change

The changes that come into the work environment with regard to the alterations in employees or the managerial structure of the company must be dealt with positively by HR. HR cannot sit and heave out a sigh, saying 'This set of recruits is a pain in the neck. The past lots were much better.'

Doing so means you have pressed the panic button in a completely inappropriate situation. The change is in the present, and you need to face—and work in—the present situation. So, when the HR professional responds positively to change, she is able to rationalize her thinking, and her vision becomes clearer and more precise. Her analytical power gets enhanced. As a result, she can turn a negative situation into a positive result.

She Must Be Flexible and Able to Adapt

This is an extension of positive response to change. A rigid inflexibility toward change in a conventional system of functioning is detrimental. Analytical reasoning in the context of human behavior cannot be thought of as a rule. HR needs to be particularly aware of this fact because few things actually happen according to conventional behavior.

For example, one employee feels happy to receive a hike in salary before the stipulated time due to excellent performance. Her productivity further increases. Likewise, this can be the case with ten other employees. But in another instance—for example, an employee dissatisfied with a managerial decision—you think it fit to allow an extended session of consultation and discussion to address the problem. It may work for one employee, but not necessarily for the next two of them. Their expectations of a solution might be completely different.

HR professionals need to be flexible in their approaches, as they are dealing with individuals and every individual is a completely different entity. Each one is unique as a result of her individual experiences and expectations. Successful HR leaders adapt to this individuality. The faster she does that, the more efficiently she can resolve issues.

She must have a thorough knowledge of the market, and this applies not only to the industry sector in which her organization operates, but also to human capital. An industry is built with the aid of its workforce, and the workforce both in and out of the HR professional's organization is a market, too. An HR professional who has a pulse of the market—that is, the status of human capital—will know the importance of keeping employees satisfied; an employee must be happy to perform well. HR is expected to go to a reasonable extent to ensure that satisfaction.

Apart from this, the market also refers to the competitive aspect of recruiting, training, and retaining the best employees. You and your organization need to climb the competitive ladder to survive. To gauge the plans and policies of competitors successfully, HR executives and departments need a sophisticated networking system, which is another example of effective public relations.

A thorough knowledge of the market ensures good prospects not only for the organization's work environment, but also for a strong competitive edge in the sector. It also goes a long way toward determining and promoting her organization's image according to the strategies devised by management.

She Must Get Along Well with Others

One of the prime responsibilities of any HR professional is to build an efficient team, so—first and foremost—she must herself be a good team member. She ought to possess an inherent quality of cooperation. This is demonstrated when she comfortably respects the individuality of the members of her team. No two people can be treated in the same way, so once each and every member feels that she is acknowledged individually, she will automatically feel comfortable and wanted. This will make the process of building a team easier.

An important point here: a sensible HR professional must not entertain the ridiculous notion that only like-minded individuals make a good team. Imagine a situation in which every member has the same response to a complex issue. How, then, is the HR professional to provide alternative solutions from which her organizational leaders may choose? For a productive environment, diverse opinions are important. A range of responsive options will enable her to analyze the advantages and drawbacks of each and choose the most appropriate solution. Yes, the team members ought to have common goals and work in unison to achieve a common mission, but they ought not all share a common process of generating and evaluating ideas.

She Must Be Independent-Minded, Diligent, and Energetic

Being a leader, the HR professional is expected to shoulder the highest burdens of responsibility and accountability. In the process of working as a team, she should always preserve her own individuality.

To arrive at an appropriate decision or an effective solution, a successful HR professional must achieve consensus among all her team members. But she must also maintain her own analysis free from any external influence or bias. Next, she must radiate energy in her style of functioning, and that energy must infuse the entire work atmosphere, so that it positively affects everyone. This will improve the productivity level of her team and the entire workforce.

An HR professional who wishes to have the maximum social impact must also be diligent in her approach. Her diligence, combined with careful attention to detail, is essential as it will instill confidence in the team and help them perform better.

She Must Be Creative and Dedicated to Achieving Goals

The HR professional must always employ an innovative approach. She should think out of the box. Making decisions based on others' observations or believing that a conventional strategy is the safest way seldom proves effective. A new approach—supported by analytical reasoning—is always appreciated and effective. Frequently, an innovative approach not only solves a particular problem but also establishes a new, positive trend in the office culture. The intention behind the act or decision is what is important

A carefully considered and honest means will definitely produce the desired end. To enhance the impact, the HR professional must have a sincere dedication in order to achieve. Her steady commitment to meeting the goal, combined with an honest, humanistic approach, can hardly be ineffective. This will help her concentrate on her goal, and he will be able to avoid distraction.

A disruption in the HR department always comes with the added challenge of distracting the team responsible for helping the entire organization achieve management's goals. It is the responsibility of the HR manager to maintain the focus of her team. This helps her identify the root cause of the problem and find an effective solution, which will—apart from solving the given problem—also remove a trail of smaller or contributing problems that may lurk in the background.

She Must Be a Dynamic Leader

Being a mere manager is not enough. The vibrancy of the HR professional must seep into her whole team. The self-motivated HR leader will increase the energy level of the workforce dramatically. She should be aware that the team members always watch her for cues from her behavior and approach. It has been noted that the team's performance is likewise affected. The attitude of the HR leader is reflected in the character of the company's workforce; therefore, the HR professional must always be completely aware of her impact and her team's.

She Must Be Responsive to Suggestions

The HR professional must be full of confidence but, at the same time, be level-headed. She must not think herself the next superwoman. When she truly values the individuality of all employees, she will respect their opinions. After all, their respective competence earned them a position on her team. The HR professional can inspire a positive attitude when she really listens to the suggestions of employees. Only when she respects employees will she be able to analyze their ideas based on merit.

The HR professional needs to make each of her employees feel comfortable as members of the team. The team members, likewise, must understand their responsibilities and be accountable for achieving them. Only then will they see fit to offer suggestions and accept suggestions from the organization's employees. To obtain the best possible ideas, the HR manager needs to educate her team members regarding her intentions, motives, and strategies, remembering that her employees are not only her most efficient brand ambassadors, but also her prime assets.

She Must Take Initiative

Being a leader, the HR professional is expected to initiate the process of working toward a desired goal. Mere ideas—no matter how brilliant—do not solve problems or foster progress. After thinking about solutions, ideas should be transformed into action. The HR executive should lead her team with wise and appropriate directives and instructions on a given plan. The leader is accountable for ensuring that team members have accurately followed directives. Any sort of ambiguity regarding the goal must be removed at all costs.

She Must Be Resourceful and Persevering

This implies that the HR leader cannot afford to be short of ideas. She is expected to be resourceful. Her innovative and creative nature will provide her with multiple options.

She ought to possess the ideas and technical knowledge to handle the different types of situations and challenges that may arise during the course of the day. It is not necessary that she have all the solutions to every problem, nor is it possible for her to devise solutions that will be effective beyond doubt. What matters is that her attitude of thinking outside of ordinary and conventional lines will equip her with multiple possible responses to a given situation.

The HR professional must also be persevering in her approach. In any given practical situation, one can only act according to the probability of success of a chosen strategy. When working with human capital, no outcome can be assured because there is no fixed rule for dealing with humans. So it is better to accept that there can be occasions when a particular HR plan or strategy might fail. The success quotient of the HR leader depends on how much her resourceful and carefully considered solutions decrease the chance of failure and on how, even if it occurs, the HR professional must not be so shocked that her sensibility abandons her.

This resilience highlights the importance of perseverance. The HR professional must learn from her failure and analyze what went wrong, striving to transform the temporary setback into a positive outcome. This can be achieved through rational analyses that stem from her self-confidence. Being the leader of the team, her attitude must always have a positive impact on her team.

She Must Be Perceptive

The HR leader is accountable for her decisions and their impacts on the company. She must, therefore, possess sufficient foresight to assess the probable outcome of her decisions and actions. It begins with the employee recruitment procedure, selecting the best candidate for the job. Every aspect of the HR professional's job demands the intricacies of a superb judgment.

A single mistake in choosing the right person for the job can result in long-term losses for the company. An incompetent employee will require greater training at the company's expense. Valuable time, energy, and money will be exhausted for extra training without any guarantee that the combined effort will have the desired result.

An employee is selected not only for her present competence and capability but also for the potential she holds for and in the company, which may be of even greater importance. Since the ultimate goal is to improve the company's growth and development, employees should have optimum potential productivity.

An effective process for filling organizational vacancies involves an innate sense of perception that helps the HR professional judge not only the right from the wrong, but also the best from the better. Perception can be increased through common sense, careful analysis, and an innovative approach.

The process of employee retention follows next. The successful retention of the best employees in the organization is an important responsibility of the HR department. Employees may decide to leave the organization for several reasons. It is the duty of the HR leader to make the working environment desirable enough that employees are convinced that it is in their best interest to stay and that the best candidates apply for vacancies when they arise. This requires a great deal of foresight.

This is also the case with the termination of service of an employee. The HR professional needs to have the foresight to gauge the possible reactions of the individual and her department. Termination is a major decision, taken only after performance coaching and careful consideration of possible alternatives. But if the HR leader fails to understand the sensitivity of the situation, a termination letter may well backfire. Grounds for legal action must be carefully considered. Decisions must be based on proper reasoning and thorough research. Sensitivity combined with practical foresight is required for the HR professional to address this difficult decision most effectively.

Therefore, perception goes a long way to help HR plan for and anticipate a positive result. HR is then also able to determine suitable solutions to the problems that may crop up—in the form of a negative reaction—because of a difficult or unpopular, but essential, decision or policy. Likewise, forethought allows the HR leader to quickly respond to unexpected reactions and prevent the situation from running out of control, thereby maintaining discipline and a positive environment in the organization.

The HR Leader Must Be Responsive to Criticism

Being an individual who has to maintain a high degree of responsibility and accountability, it is only natural that the HR professional will receive some negative feedback and comments. Her decisions might not find equal favor throughout the organization. At no point can the HR leader forget that she is dealing with humans and that every individual thinks about things her own way.

It is inevitable that some decisions from HR will find disfavor; criticism will follow. A successful and competent HR manager will not be angered or disheartened by those criticisms. In fact, such a negative response from her would increase discontent, and the work atmosphere would be adversely affected

Criticism is frequently a valuable source of feedback. It helps an individual stand on a firm, level ground and prevents dangerous overconfidence. It makes her aware of the fact that no one is perfect and—however capable she might be—she can be wrong. She also needs to realize that there is always room for improvement. Being a people's profession, HR is dynamic and ever-changing.

It actually makes sense for the HR manager to take this criticism as a learning experience and review her decision or a given situation. More often than not, she will discover a detail or unexpected result that she had overlooked or ignored. Not only does criticism give her the chance to analyze before a bigger problem emerges, but it can act as a buffer for critical situations and give her valuable time to correct a mistake.

Therefore, it can be said that the work entrusted to the HR leader has far-reaching and positive impacts. The HR professional is the architect responsible for the development and overall shaping of the organization. A competent HR manager exerts the maximum effort to succeed in achieving the organization's goals. The vast range of effort that she undertakes is an attempt to make these goals a reality.

But have you ever come across any organization that continuously sings the praises of its HR department's efforts? I do not think so. Nor does the HR manager continuously receive praise. This is the reason I call the HR functional approach and ideals a noble pedestal.

The HR professional works diligently and positively but without any expectation of recognition or reward. She does it in a style of community service. She does it because she loves the job. The growth and development of the company is the sole reward for which she is working.

The manner in which she deals with human capital reflects her intent to serve employees and the community at large. Her approach is such that employees receive the maximum possible benefit and grow along with the company. I call it nobility personified. Only an individual who is in real love with this work can be a successful HR professional!

She weaves the tight fabric of in-house relationships, memories, dreams, and shared willingness to invest and sacrifice for an even better future for the individuals in her organization. Our modern society is faced with depression, addiction, illiteracy, divorce, and despair to mention only a few challenges. Even a cursory observation reveals that the HR leader is on the front line of all these personal battles.

The issues she deals with are, in fact, a by-product of the different manifestations of these battles. Say, a depressed employee lacks motivation, a victim of whatever sort of addiction lacks the spirit to perform, a victim of family violence lacks confidence, and so on. The various initiatives taken by the HR discipline and the different support systems adopted by it during the last two to three decades offers the much-needed chance for the workforce to overcome personal challenges and succeed through work.

CHAPTER 4

BUILDING TRUST

THE PRIME TRUST-BUILDER BETWEEN MANAGEMENT AND EMPLOYEES

The HR professional is the mediator and the interlocutor between the organization's executive team and the organization's employees. In many instances, she is the sole medium of communication between them. Management makes a certain decision and hands over the responsibility to formulate the policy and execute it successfully to the HR department.

Management must have complete confidence in the HR department in order to entrust it with these essential responsibilities. Likewise, employees should also feel comfortable and at ease communicating with the HR department about their individual issues or company policies. The bridge of trust between management and employees must always be open and free from any distracting obstructions.

As with every relationship, the one between management, HR, and employees is built on trust. To foster this reciprocal commitment, there are a few essential responsibilities:

- The HR professional must be aware of and understand the methods critical to building this relationship of trust.
- The HR professional must also be conscious of the biases and prejudices inherent in all people that make us distrust people.
- The HR professional must know how to repair trust when necessary.

- The HR professional must understand and uphold the importance of the organizational perspective in nurturing and developing this trust.

WHAT IS TRUST?

Trust is acting toward another individual or group of individuals in a manner that conveys their integrity, dependability, and benevolence. The process has two aspects that the HR leader must work on consistently and constantly:

- Express positive expectations for the other's behavior and intentions.
- Send messages that encourage the confidence of the person on whom the trust is bestowed.

The HR department is regularly on the lookout for new tools that will enable them to build this trust. In HR, this is a relatively traditional topic. But in today's rapidly changing world of business, a new set of proactive HR planning tools are required so that the HR department can meet the new challenges and improve the organization's competitive advantage.

These are a particular set of plans for HR to follow:

The Corporate Head Count

The head count is also called the Fat Assessment Plan. Successful HR leaders need a set of assessment tools to track the head count in all departments and analyze where overhead costs may be excessive.

Redeployment Plan

These are also called agility plans. The present market is dynamic, and the successful HR manager must devise and constantly update her strategy to remain agile by shifting people and resources swiftly from low-return areas to high-return areas.

The "Smoke Detectors"

A proactive HR professional must be able to anticipate problems. Developing the HR system and metrics is called "smoke detectors," because they indicate potential problems, giving you enough time to devise plans and strategies to avert the problem entirely or—at least—to minimize its negative impact.

The Back Fill Plan

This is also called the "bench strength" plan. Because employees occasionally and inevitably leave, it is important to have a strategy in place to identify and develop individuals who can assume that employee's responsibilities. But one must not confuse back fill plans with succession plans. Traditional succession planning applies only to the key jobs within a particular department. It is the responsibility of individual managers to develop at least one individual to fill every key job.

The Employee Challenge Plan

Employees leave their jobs mostly due to a lack of challenge in the workplace. According to this plan, individual managers need to develop "challenge plans" for every employee under the supervisor. The result should be a dramatic increase in retention rates. This plan requires a monthly review to ensure that each individual enjoys constant growth and feels challenged.

The Retention Plan

Retention planning is an important corporate strategy to decrease turnover. The first step requires the identification of key performers and the positions that are hard to fill. The at-risk individuals are also identified. Position-wise, strategy plans are then developed to increase retention rates. Proper research is conducted to find out why people remain in or leave their jobs.

The Horizontal Progression Plan

Today, most companies are de-layered. A lot of management positions have been eliminated. So, there is little opportunity to stimulate employees through promotion. Companies, therefore, need to practice job rotation plans or horizontal transfers to promote technical and managerial skills among the employees they hope to retain and turn into future leaders.

Work-Life Balance Forecasts

With an increasing demand for a wide assortment of benefits and work-life balance options for employees, it is imperative for the HR department to work out strategies that will enable it to forecast those options in advance. This will also help the department anticipate how employees would take advantage of work-life balance programs like job sharing and sabbaticals.

A Learning/Knowledge Plan

The HR manager can develop individual and corporate learning plans to improve the art of learning and the effective application of that knowledge in furthering the company's productivity. This ensures competitive advantage, since the company can acquire information or solutions quickly and distribute it throughout the company at an even greater speed.

Skills/Competency Inventories

HR needs to develop skill or competency inventories to redistribute resources and plug unexpected vacancies quickly and efficiently. These inventories would allow them to apply the best possible talent to any particular challenge, as the HR department would already be aware of those individuals within the organization who have the competence and experience to solve a particular problem. People will not be required to move between positions because they are solely the source of advice and benchmarking.

The Interest Inventories

The needs and expectations of employees are constantly changing. HR needs to have the strategy to identify and meet changing requirements. It is essential to retain the organization's best employees. HR can ask employees directly about projects that they might like to work on, the special skills that they would like to develop, or the individual or team that they would like to work with. All these answers will equip HR with the necessary information. Apart from increasing worker engagement, such questions will also increase their productivity levels.

The HR Competitive Analysis

The principle of devising an ideal HR strategy is to become superior when compared to the company's direct competitors. Conducting regular comparative strategy assessments is vital. Apart from this, to make the improvement consistent, HR has the option of reporting details in comparison to preceding years.

The Bad Management Identification Program

The number one reason employees quit their jobs is poor management by their immediate supervisors. It is the HR department's responsibility to address this challenge, therefore, these faulty management styles and techniques must be identified and resolved with immediate effect through training, transfer, or release. After all, HR is responsible for meeting employees' requirements. So, regular communication with employees, offering them challenging and interesting tasks and simultaneously recognizing and appreciating their efforts can go a long way to increase productivity levels and achieve a sharp decrease in turnover.

Develop Targeted Succession Plans

These are narrowly focused strategies to ensure that competent employees are constantly available for possible vacancies in important project teams. Succession plans often fail because they are too broad. So, plans needs to be focused so the forecast becomes more specific and accurate.

The Turnover or Exit Forecast

With the state of major economies of the world constantly fluctuating, accurate predictions for the supply of labor become quite difficult. HR needs to be aware of the costs that the company will incur in the form of loss of talent through either turnover or retirement. So, plans needs to be developed accordingly so that the company will be least affected by these losses. This can be achieved through proper recruitment or internal promotions in the organization.

AN IDEAL MODEL OF TRUST:

Trust can be defined as an individual's state of readiness to interact with someone or something without any defense mechanism. An ideal model of trust consists of three components:

1. The capacity for individuals to trust other individuals and the organization
2. The perception of competence
3. The perception of intentions

A capacity to trust derives from an individual's experiences in life and her expectations and experiences of risk. The perception of competence requires the perception of her own ability and the ability of her coworkers to perform and succeed in a given situation. The perception of intentions indicates the perception an individual has that the actions, words, direction, mission, and decisions are motivated by mutually-serving instead of self-serving motives. These three components make the understanding of trust easier.

To see the importance of trust in a work environment, we can refer to Aristotle's *Rhetoric*, in which he states that the trust of the speaker in his listener was based on the listener's perception of the three characteristics of the speaker.

1. Reliability—the competence factor
2. Honesty—the measure of his intentions

3. The good will of the speaker—her favorable intention in the direction of the listener

Trust is a necessary precondition for having faith in an individual, fostering cooperation and promoting team spirit, undertaking well-calculated and worthy risks, and enhancing credible and effective communication.

To promote trust in the work environment, HR should take care not to diminish trust in the first place. The integrity of all employees' leadership is critical in the progress of the organization. A leader's truthfulness and transparency in communicating with her coworkers is equally important. The strength of her vision and commitment to the organization's unifying mission can promote a trustworthy environment. Whereas, trust can be potentially broken when a communication is misunderstood or an order is misdirected.

Building a trust-based relationship takes intense action. HR should undertake the endeavor with the desire to build an empowering and spirited work environment. But, without honest intent, it is simply a farce and a deception. People have an uncanny ability to understand the difference, which can cause the HR professional to lose her most valuable asset: the trust of her employees.

Trust in an organization not only improves the work environment but also makes targets comfortably achievable. Trust not only fosters effective communication, employee retention and motivation, and contribution of unrestricted energy but also encourages the voluntary extra effort that employees invest in their careers and the company.

Every minute action is accountable for developing trust. According to Marsha Sinetar, the author of *Can You Simply Trust?* "Trust is not a matter of technique, but of character; we are trusted because of our way of being, not because of our polished exteriors or our expertly crafted communications."

Therefore, trust is the fundamental building block for the development of the organization's future. It is HR's responsibility to lay the foundations. Building trust entails telling the difficult truths and being authentic and worthy of commitment while dealing with employees, management, and customers alike. It is simultaneously profoundly rewarding and the ultimate service mission.

CHAPTER 5

HR—WHERE CREDIBILITY RULES

DELIVERING BEYOND EXPECTATIONS

The concept of credibility in the HR profession is a two-fold combination, consisting of personal and systematic credibility. **Personal credibility** involves standing up for oneself and one's department, while **systematic credibility** involves the use of different tools and techniques that will advance the credibility factor and buy-in of the other aspects of the organization.

The leadership credibility of the HR professional is very important. People naturally obey and follow a credible leader. As a leader, the HR professional needs to be charismatic and compelling in justifying her approach. Any robust organization cannot afford to have an HR professional who lacks these qualities. The everyday parlances of the HR strategy involve jumping into the world of metrics and quantification and solving people-based problems with an analytical approach combined with a human touch. Employees cannot succeed under an HR leader who is a party to her own powerlessness.

The new millennium requires HR to think persistently and urgently about the future. The department needs to properly chart strategies and envision, prioritize, and set goals for the future.

The credibility factor is determined by the following factors for HR:

- The HR manager is a strategic partner.
- Her strategies emanate from the business' strategies.

- The competitive environment has enhanced the importance of the HR role.
- The growing impact of information technology has enabled new forms of HR planning.
- The imminent scarcity of qualified employees
- The training and development of employees
- The major functions that include performance appraisals, skills enhancement, and planning benefits and compensation need continual improvement
- The increasing emergence of knowledgeable employees

To understand the importance of credibility in the functions of HR, a comparative study of the changing role of the HR discipline in the recent years was conducted. Previously, the factors that determined success were simple business understanding, judgment, and intuition. Currently, those factors include three elements: accurate information, an effective strategic plan, and a focused mission. But the HR leader must have in mind that the success criteria for the future are flexibility, agility, and speed.

The organizational style of the company was paternalistic. The HR department had a similar approach. Today, the approach is more impartial and professional. The future style of functioning is slated to be more oriented toward empowering individuals with strategic application of technology and training to emphasize expectations of—and tools for—independent thinking and action.

In the past, employees were considered 'hungry, naked, and defenseless creatures.' The reasons for such a perception of employees were stagnant or negligible economic growth and a social hierarchy. Today's competent employees are the direct product of vibrant economic growth and social liberalization. Therefore, they are naturally thought of as thinking and rational beings, and organizations acknowledge and respect their individuality. In the near future, employees are likely to develop as mature, fully evolved, and satisfied human beings.

The motivational methods in the organization used to simply drive employees through their basic requirements. Today, employees are walked through social and intellectual requirements on behalf of the company. Future employees are expected to be self-motivated.

The role of the HR department in the past was merely to provide workers with the means to acquire the minimum necessities of life. Today, employees need to be motivated through effective and reasonable performance appraisals and compensation systems. In the future, HR leaders are likely to act as change agents, innovators, and strategic partners.

These comparisons reveal the degree to which credibility has influenced these changes. Time has increased the credibility factor. The HR manager has evolved into more of a natural leader, responsible and accountable for the initiation and implementation of changes effectively throughout the organization. With the progression of society and the resulting improvement in the standard of living, the role of HR professionals as traditional motivators has also changed.

According to behavioral sciences, people accept the decisions that positively affect their well-being. So, the credibility of the modern HR manager lies in how well she is able to plan various strategies and develop policies to direct employees along the desired path. That means that it is the responsibility of the HR manager to ensure that her employees do not consider their position to be boring, monotonous, or uninspiring. It is the end goal—which must be significant enough and effectively planned by the HR department—that makes even a dreary task exciting.

Team spirit has gradually gained importance with time. Not long ago, team-building was seen as parallel to employee organizing, which made management suspicious. The mere idea of getting together as a team suggested that the employees were planning outrageous actions against management. Today, with the socioeconomic development in almost every country, the concept of employees as hapless creatures has been fundamentally and irrevocably altered.

With the increase in the status of individual employees, today's employees have gained something their predecessors never had: confidence. A competent employee is confident about her position as well as her qualifications. Management has also realized that it is in the best interest of the company for individuals to work as a team.

The corporate style has changed and successful teamwork is given more recognition than solitary achievement. Dynamic teams always create motivated, creative people who take pleasure in self-expression. The entire process enhances job satisfaction as a natural result of organizational growth.

In the present day, successful HR leaders and departments have evolved into an entity that employees can believe in and trust. They feel confident and satisfied working under its leadership. As employees' productivity level increases, a better understanding develops between management and employees because HR works as a reliable medium of communication between them. Therefore, today's challenge for a successful HR professional is building and enhancing this credibility.

THE CREDIBILITY FACTOR IS BROUGHT HOME BY THE VERY STYLE AND METHOD OF HR FUNCTIONING.

It begins with employee recruitment, staffing, skill development, motivation, and other general HR practices. HR must be thoroughly updated with new technological improvements that are in direct relation to working with human capital. One must remember that HR is no longer about handing over a set of stringent company rules and a monotonous work schedule to an employee who has no promise for substantial development.

Today, successful HR departments have no choice but to deliver beyond expectation. The credibility factor comes into play here. Plans, strategies, and goals must be made clear to all employees. They ought to know exactly what they are working for. It will not only help to maintain focus and strategize effectively but also lift the veil of secrecy between statement and intent. The ultimate result of progress and development will be achieved naturally.

This credibility challenge is fulfilled through the following HR functions:

- recruiting people with multidimensional experiences and skills;
- infusing fresh blood in the organization at regular intervals;
- developing an appealing work culture; and
- anticipating vacancies that do not yet exist and identifying competent candidates before those vacancies actually arise

All the above functions can be effectively carried out when the HR manager hones her credibility skills by taking initiative in developing self-expressed individualism within her employees; and enabling and facilitating their effective participation in team-building

EMOTIONAL INTELLIGENCE

This is the principle factor that determines credibility. HR works with human capital, and—however analytical and rational we think we are—at the end of the day, we are all emotional creatures. A successful and credible HR manager acknowledges and takes care of her employees' emotional requirements. An HR manager can be well-trained in her responsibilities, can have a highly insightful and analytical mind full of innovative ideas, but unless her IQ is combined with a high EQ, she will not become a natural leader.

A high correlation has always been observed between emotional intelligence and effective performance.

People with high emotional intelligence are characterized by:
- an ability to foster great interpersonal relations;
- independence and independent thinking;
- self-motivation;
- an emphatic nature; and
- a tendency to be self-controlled and -directed;

Now, take a look at the following points—according to a survey by Dr. Reuven Baron, author of The Handbook of Emotional Intelligence, who surveyed over 500,000 individuals across the globe,—which reveal the importance of emotional intelligence in the corporate world:
- Emotional intelligence has been proven to be twice as important as any other job-related factors.
- Star performers possess comparatively higher emotional intelligence capabilities than their lower-performing colleagues.
- More than 90 percent of those star performers attribute their success to emotional intelligence rather than other cognitive factors

Proper balance between ones' work life and personal life is an important aspect in every professional's life. The HR manager needs to acknowledge this. To cater to efficiency in the organization, HR must adopt an approach that synchronizes these two priorities.

THE CHANGE ADVOCATE

HR professionals must also work as "change advocates," which refers to the factors that foster change in employees' individual behaviors. A successful and effective change advocate has to be an extrovert equipped with impressive interpersonal skills. She must be highly innovative, be willing to take risks, and possess strong organizational capability.

To be a good change advocate, the HR professional must possess the following characteristics:

Homophily—This refers to the degree of closeness and similarity between the employee and management. The goal should be to enhance the closeness of this relationship. The closer it is, the easier and more successful the change.

Empathy—The HR manager ought to be sensitive to the feelings of employees. She should understand their thoughts and emotions. She must be sincere in her intent. The result is improved communication between the employee and management, which makes change easier.

Proximity—This enables easy access between both parties.

Structure and Organization—She must have a proper and clear planning of all activities are related to a change. Well-devised strategies make change easier.

Openness—A reasonable amount of transparency contributes to an effective outcome of strategies or programs.

Reward—It is natural for employees to expect change to result in benefits for them. The HR professional should plan rewards for both the short-term and the long-term. It is important to inform employees about these rewards, too.

STRATEGIC PARTNER

The HR manager is a strategic partner who assists in the organization's development. To succeed in this role, she is required to possess the following qualities:

- She must have sound knowledge of business, as well as HR, functions.
- She must be capable of leading the change process and be innovative and resourceful in solving problems.
- She must possess the natural leadership to influence on and persuade the organization toward certain matters that will increase the potential for success.

THE HUMAN TOUCH

An atmosphere that is conducive to trust and teamwork fosters an enhanced quality of life at work. This is essential for promoting progress in an organization, because it builds an environment that has excellent interpersonal relations together with highly motivated employees who are willing to put in their maximum effort to achieve the company's goals. Although many business leaders believe that monetary benefits are the primary motivating factors, HR leaders will make sure not to ignore several other factors such as job restructuring and redesign, career and personal development, and promotional opportunities to name just a few.

A successful human capital operation is never possible without the human touch. It is HR's responsibility to take care of the organization's human capital. So the aspects of an employee's job that determine motivation also require a human touch in every style and approach. Until recently, employees changed jobs for a better salary, but today, they look for something beyond salary. This is the reason the majority of companies devise attractive nonfinancial benefits.

Celebrations and ceremonies can be a great way to add the human touch. The organization can celebrate achievements by teams and individuals.

HR could also provide birthday gifts and dinner coupons on marriage anniversaries of employees.

Other possible benefits could include flexible work days or work weeks, paid vacations, appreciation letters or cards to recognize individual achievement, an outing for a project team after successful completion of a project; or desirable canteen facilities and modern recreation rooms.

The credibility of the HR manager can be effectively enhanced if she functions by the following guidelines:

- She should be accurate in everything under her jurisdiction.
- Her style of management must be consistent and predictable; she should not make decisions that strike employees as being out of the blue.
- She must meet commitments and take responsibility for the successful completion of her programs within specified budgets and time periods.

- She must possess a high personal comfort level with her colleagues, superiors, and subordinates.

With a huge amount of human potential untapped, the human being is frequently the organization's most underutilized resource. HR managers deal with human capital, so to enhance their credibility and develop an appropriate environment, they need to feel the pulse of this human spirit. Their ability to harness that latent potential is the sole determinant of either the success or the failure of their organizations.

HR—THE CREDIBLE ACTIVIST

With the continuous evolution of business and management disciplines, the style and approach of the HR manager must also constantly evolve. Her skills and expertise must be an embodiment of sophistication to create a perfect recipe for success. The Human Resource Competency Study (HRCS), carried out in 2007 by Dave Ulrich and Wayne Brockbank, claims that the HR professional is expected to deliver outstanding performance if she is to be considered a "credible activist."

As the name suggests, a credible activist must be both credible and proactive. In being credible, she must be able to keep commitments, thus cultivating respect and admiration. She also ought to be proactive in the sense that she must possess her own point of view, challenge assumptions, initiate action, and work toward successful realization of goals.

A credible activist can redirect her skills and expertise to culminate in competency in some other important areas, including:

- **Becoming a Culture and Change Steward**
  Culture must not be misinterpreted as being a single event; it is a consistent pattern across assorted activities. A company serves its external customers, and the concept of culture originates in a clear understanding of the expectations these customers have. Culture helps to relate those expectations to the internal employees and, thus, translate them into organizational behavior. This makes achievement of customers' expectations possible.

    Therefore, a successful HR professional must have the ability to create the culture and devise disciplinary methods to drive required changes in the company. With proper implementation of strategies, initiatives, and projects, the HR professional will achieve credibility.

- **Becoming an Organizational Designer and Talent Manager**
  The HR manager should effectively learn, understand, and practice the theories of talent management and organizational design. The entire process—beginning with the recruitment of the new employees through their training and development and gradual promotions, along with their movement across departmental boundaries or perhaps out of the company—constitutes talent management.

  Organizational design involves the structure, processes, and policies that give shape to the working style of the company. It defines the capability of the company with respect to all the previously mentioned factors. Good talent is complementary to the development of the organization. Good talent in an unsupportive company is unsustainable, and a good organization without proper talent will simply not deliver.

- **Becoming Strategy Architects**
  HR professionals ought to have a vision of the company's prospects for the future. They must play a very active role in the overall strategy development for future success. This involves identifying and incorporating new business trends and their potential impact on the business. HR professionals must also be able to predict the obstacles that might interfere with the realization of success.

- **Becoming Operational Executors**
  HR professionals must be comfortable and competent in the execution of operational aspects within the organization. These include routine jobs such as drafting, adapting, and implementing policies. They must have an eye for the basic requirements of all employees, including salaries, training, redeployment, and, of course, recruitment and retention.

- **Becoming Business Allies of the Company**
  An HR professional can become a proficient business ally. She needs to be aware of the social context and setting of the industries in which the company operates. Only then will she contribute to the success of the business. A sound knowledge

of customers' unique needs will help her understand the reason they buy the company's services or products. Moreover, since the HR professional is expected to have a basic understanding of the functions of the different corporate departments (finance, marketing, sales, R&D, etc.), she can surely help the business add to the bottom line.

This range of essential complementary qualities in the HR professional increases her credibility quotient as she works for the benefit of employees and management alike. Then she is more often than not found to deliver beyond normal expectations. Thanks to her sensitivity, resourcefulness, innovation, and self-confidence, improvement in the longitudinal waves of her performance graph increases her credibility. She becomes the person of choice for both management and employees.

The fundamental principle of HR is to initiate an atmosphere of positivism and create profound and lasting change to maintain that atmosphere. According to researches, five important ingredients are required for any development initiative and for augmenting positive transformation. Each of these ingredients is necessary, and they offer results in combination—not one is sufficient in isolation.

1. The HR professional needs to possess a distinct clarity of vision that consists of both the present reality and the possible reality. She must work toward promoting the development of this vision.
2. The HR professional is the support source for employees. She issues directives, so, her support must be both structural and emotional. She needs to not merely offer but also develop the support.
3. She must be clear about the sort of change that she desires. Likewise, she should develop the relevant knowledge and skills to ensure the desired change. She must possess the capability to reflect on the utility of the desired change.
4. She must develop a systems perspective and function accordingly. The comprehensiveness, reliability, and configuration should be the major areas of her concern.

5. The desired or proposed transformation must be supported with the use of ample stories or the development of art, images, and rituals.

THE IMPORTANCE OF BEING A CREDIBLE ACTIVIST

HR professionals are usually subject matter experts capable of coming up with advice whenever required. However, expertise is not enough to ensure the success of HR. To become a key part of management, the HR professional ought to be more than just a specialist.

What is required is her ability to stamp her individual mark on important issues or decisions, possess the courage to challenge assumptions about conventional methods, and the ability and analytical judgment to take smart risks in the face of probable opportunities. Therefore, she must have credibility as an expert in her field and be an activist who initiates positive change.

Becoming a credible activist can bring about a significant change in an HR professional's style of functioning, and for some, it might mean a simple redevising of her operating style. In either case, this unfolds a new dimension of the HR profession. The bottom line is, instead of waiting to be asked by company management to respond on a certain issue, the HR activist proactively presents the CEO with suggestions and action plans. Her innovative approach may involve certain risks, but she stands a good chance of succeeding if she knows her basics.

THE BENEFITS OF BEING A CREDIBLE ACTIVIST

Being a credible activist can be of immense help to both the HR professional and the company. It does not make sense to only attend to human resource issues. A proactive broadening of perspective is required to respond to issues that really need attention.

Credible activism demonstrates to the company's executive team that the HR manager is a worthy and capable leader. She is thought of as someone who realizes and identifies important issues for the organization and who offers solutions and accomplishes the desired goals.

The credible activist becomes all important because the HR professional works with people—business involves problems, and problems involve people. The people being the "stock in trade" of the

HR professional, a strong HR management team is essential. That team will apply its vibrancy and dynamism to accomplish feats throughout the company, touching on:

- employee/labor relations;
- company-wide goal alignment;
- multidisciplinary and multilevel teamwork;
- qualitative improvement resulting from calculated risk; and
- increased creativity and problem-solving.

Until recently, the work of the HR professional was viewed as an essentially backroom transactional function. Today, she has become a vital part of the company's competitive edge. Basically, the organization's intellectual capital, human endowment, intangibles, and capabilities are all derived from the competence and commitment of its human resource professionals.

So the HR leader must not only know how to get things done but also have the ability to apply her knowledge across organizational boundaries. Her credibility factor is enhanced as she becomes increasingly adept in new areas of competency.

The HR professional is required to be credible and active at the same time. Trust, respect, admiration, and obedience should follow her naturally. Her sense of individualism, confidence, authority, and management constitute the other important qualifications. If the HR professional is credible but not proactive, she will always fail to have an impact. And those HR professionals who are not credible but have ideas will not be listened to at all.

Statistical studies reveal that, with the availability of proper training and awareness, more than sixty percent of today's HR professionals can adopt this vital and essential skill. But, around twenty percent in the HR world do not have either the necessary skills or the personality to develop this talent.

How Is Credibility Established?

Credibility is achieved through the attainment of results.

Meeting Commitments

The HR professional must stand by the commitments she undertakes. Her each and every step must be characterized by integrity.

Relationship Management

The successful HR professional must have the innate ability to build strong, trust-based relationships with her employees. She must have a wonderful working relationship with line managers, executives, consultants, vendors, and customers. This enables her to identify, address, and resolve interpersonal problems within the organization. The atmosphere, therefore, will not threaten the productivity of the company. What's more, she will be admired for it.

Communication Skills

Effective communication is always better than flowery but incomprehensible or irrelevant communication. In addition to communicating effectively with individuals on a personal level, the HR professional must productively interact with a large and diverse group of people inside and outside her organization.

Words Complemented by Action

Important HR and company messages must be communicated with both words and actions. The essential actions—like recruitment, promotion, reward, or training of employees—must be articulated clearly and properly throughout the company. Moreover, the messages that are intended to engage employees in and align them with a specific cause must be clearly communicated to achieve crucial HR and company goals.

Tenacity and Commitment

Personal credibility is effectively established through tenacity and commitment. The HR professional is expected to possess excellent interpersonal skills, along with a record of delivering on her obligations. Not only that, she must also be able to communicate quantifiable outcomes accurately. Consistently performing and meeting her commitments goes a long way toward enhancing her credibility. Without these qualities, she is liable to be excluded from strategic decisions and activities of the organization.

As such, personal credibility stands on a high pedestal. Today's HR professionals are required to invent and replenish their skills, devise new strategies, and plug possible cracks in the system. Their own credibility allows them to demand the same level of integrity and commitment from employees. Every HR professional in today's corporate world, from the new graduate to the seasoned specialist, can enhance her contribution to her company by increasing her personal credibility. A credible HR professional is able to offer her organization the complete value of the available human capital.

Credibility, Competence, and Compassion (the Three C's of HR) form the building blocks of a successful HR career. When promises are kept, trust is built and credibility is created. Honesty, openness, and strict follow-through ensure credibility. The employee and the organization trust the HR professional when she 'walks the walk,' meaning that her communication and her actions are in perfect harmony. Through credibility, HR builds relationships and reputation.

The objectives that enhance HR credibility include:

- Appropriately balancing organizational requirements and staff concerns;
- Protecting the company from liability without treating employees as potential plaintiffs;
- Persistently influencing employee actions and behavior without exerting excessive control; and
- Not making herself a rule-maker or an obstacle-creator, rather attempting to be perceived and appreciated as a resource, mentor, and educator.

The HR professional should take care not to promote a separation between management and employees. She should be an ally in the work culture; her mission will be easier to accomplish. HR should be subtle and considerate in management procedures. Remember, this is a new generation at HR's disposal, and members of that generation do not like to be managed.

Credibility will increase exponentially when employees realize that, through the work culture the HR professional is promoting, she is helping her employees to become good managers and leaders.

HR's style of management should not seem like an undesirable external interference. The department is promoting a work culture, so it should be a part of it. Employees will appreciate that HR shares a similar work life with them. This is "management in a residential situation," in which the HR leader is alongside employees—actually or virtually—almost 24/7. But the HR professional should not merely work with them, she should try to live as they do.

She should also help employees realize the importance of their work. This can be easily done by making them feel valuable to the organization. HR has recruited them because of their competence. Therefore, it is now HR's responsibility to nurture them and enable them to flourish. The HR professional will be earnestly thanked for her efforts to this end.

Another method of credibility enhancement is the propagation of a system of rewards. If an employee improves her performance, HR should praise her for her achievement. When the outcome is intangible—say, an educational or academic achievement—and the employee finds herself acknowledged, she feels good and her future performance is positively affected.

In the modern corporate environment, employees behave as though they work in a company on a transitional basis. Among factors contributing to turnover among such employees are dissatisfaction with the job, an unhappy or uncomfortable work environment, incompetent supervisors, lack of challenge, and no chance for intellectual growth.

So HR needs to look at the stability in the work environment and take care of all the factors related to employee satisfaction. The process of recruitment and training must be stable and continuous.

Employees come from different social and cultural backgrounds, so their common platform is their qualification and their work competency. After they join the organization, it is the HR leader's responsibility to encourage the development of a human bond among the entire organization of employees. She needs to acknowledge the individuality of each employee, along with each employee's objectives and desired career path. HR is required to promote the feeling that all of them stand on a level platform and are a team with a common mission: the development and progress of the organization to which they belong.

They need to be convinced that their individual progress is directly related to the progress of the company. A clarification of the objective and mission in a friendly and "one among yourself" manner supplements credibility with the competence of HR.

Certain common behavioral patterns have been found to have a negative impact on the credibility of HR. They are credibility-destroying actions:

Acting as an Apologist for Management

There can be instances when a particular decision or an action of management goes wrong. At those times, it is sensible and wise for HR to admit the mistake. HR should then work toward undoing the change or reversing the unworkable policy or decision. HR should never act like a toady and simply jump on the next boat sailing through. She will only earn contempt if she does that.

Cynically Approaching Employees and Their Concerns

Employees are neither machines nor robots nor are they the company's bonded laborers. They are individuals with individual problems and concerns. HR should not give them a cold look when they present their problems. The HR professional should judge a problem on the basis of its justification in relation to the work profile. A cynical attitude that all employees are potential troublemakers will damage HR's credibility.

Labeling employees as complainers may cause an HR professional to overlook potential dangers disguised as only a tiny problem. Your failure to listen to valid concerns will not only alienate you from employees but also prevent you from taking important corrective measures.

Failing to Be Aware of Important Changes in the Law

Legal issues are very case sensitive. The smallest change or alteration can have far-reaching effects and unintended repercussions. HR must keep an eye on the legal protection of the company.

Trying to Be a Cop Instead of a Consultant

As mentioned earlier, the HR professional is most effective and appreciated when she does not overtly exercise control over employees. She should avoid acting bossy and place herself on a level plane with her employees. Under usual circumstances, employees consider the HR manager to be their leader, and she needs to ensure the maximum positive results and without losing the good faith of the employees she serves.

Not Keeping Employee Confidences

A gossip does not belong in the work profile of today's HR professionals. They should deal with problems and make an earnest effort to solve them. Because an HR leader's responsibilities include employees' problems and cover all the human capital, she will inevitably encounter personal challenges in her employees' lives.

She ought to behave like a kind confidant. She should realize that the concerned employee has revealed her secret in the hope of having the problem resolved.

Gossiping must be treated as a cardinal sin. A breach of confidence has the potential to inflict irreparable damage to the credibility of the HR manager and department for years to come.

Focusing on the Turf Instead of the Mission

The HR manager is a proactive policy enforcer but is required to work in tandem with management and the workforce alike. She is not only the medium of change but also the building block of company progress; this is a huge responsibility. She cannot afford to be selfish in her approach if she wants to be credible and successful.

Since she needs to maintain a healthy balance, she cannot be more interested in protecting her bastion of power than in the selfless discharge of her duties—promoting the company interests is paramount. Her mission should reign supreme when she is working with employees.

When she is more interested in protecting her own interests, employees naturally think of her as a selfish individual who is only interested in promoting an image. Her attempts to enforce a selfless work culture are ignored.

A credible HR manager is required, first and foremost, to lead by example. Employees take the signal of work culture from her. No one can earn respect when she preaches one thing and does one thing.

Additionally, the HR manager ought to avoid creating a situation in which employees feel that HR is the only source of corporate information. Employees should feel comfortable finding management information from other sources than the HR department. Otherwise, they may conclude that it is a demonstration of the HR leader's insecurity. They may also think that you want to limit the education of employees and that you do not want certain information passed down to them.

The HR manager loses credibility if employees think there is a motivation behind her action that is not in their favor. Transparency in the work culture is negatively affected, which inevitably spells doom not just for the HR department but, of course, for the organization as a whole.

The bottom line is, therefore, that the HR professional must be credible and competent at the same time. It is more important for her to do right than to be right. When the HR department has the guts and the insight to maintain the work standard designed for the company's progress, she needs to stand her ground even if it means walking away from the job. This can occur in extreme conditions and is not rare for an ideal HR professional—she is the essence of credibility.

It is not only a personal moral achievement, but also an important lesson for your employees. Such an action makes the company to consider the opinion that led to the disagreement.

If an HR professional is willing to go to any length to hold on to her job, then she can be sure that she has already begun her long walk down a smooth and grassy surface that leads to a fiery and hopeless prison.

THE HR PROFESSIONAL'S CREDIBILITY LEADS HER TO BECOME A BUSINESS PARTNER

Of all the formal processes and practices of the HR department, credibility is the most potent factor that contributes to the business partnerships within the company.

Trust, respect, dependence and confidence are the natural outcomes of this equation. The combination of that assortment is sure to deliver tangible returns to the organization, securing and enhancing the strategic partnership between HR and the company. It is an important transition of HR's role from being a service provider to a strategic business partner. This is the highest measure of any HR professional's competence. She enjoys the satisfaction of a higher level of contribution and attains a position from which she can further demonstrate her worth.

This is possible through an understanding of the larger context of meeting the company's objectives. Her entrepreneurial approach to service delivery gains recognition.

Ultimately, the credibility of the HR function lives and dies on its ability to generate customer satisfaction—or, deliver a service that meets customer expectations. That is the only desired criteria from the corporate point of view.

CHAPTER 6

HR MANAGER: THE EXPERT SOCIALIZER

TRAINING AND INSTRUCTING EMPLOYEES WITHOUT BRUISING THEIR EGOS

The HR manager works with human capital, which involves dealing with people who have their own attributes, attitudes and personalities. To ensure the maximum productivity level among the workforce, management should ensure that employees are comfortable enough to put in their best work.

She must instigate and maintain a work culture that enhances the feeling of comfort among employees. Socializing greatly promotes this comfort level, and increase in comfort level automatically increases the productivity of the company.

Effective socializing is a medium through which new recruits become accustomed to the existing work environment. They are methodically introduced to the work culture. The main objective is to improve relationships and promote teamwork. In a lighter vein and in an easy and comfortable atmosphere, recruits learn the rules, regulations and ethics of the organization.

Overt exercise of control and regulation seldom produces effective results, because employees find their individuality under threat, and it is pretty obvious that no self-respecting individual will like it. The moment disgust and resentment begins to develop in the office culture, it fosters negativity in the entire system.

Therefore, individual egos should be well taken care of under reasonable limitations and with respect to work ethics. The entire training and instruction procedure can be carried out in a comfortable atmosphere to attain optimum results.

In the majority of companies nowadays, management invests a lot of time, money, and effort in the process of planning, promoting, and even sponsoring social events for employees. For example, companies create a social committee that is responsible for arranging various social activities. Holiday parties and picnics can be sponsored to show appreciation for hard-working employees and act as a morale booster.

These events perform a dual function. Being work-sponsored events, on one hand, they serve business purposes, and on the other hand, they come across as social functions for employees' entertainment. A few guidelines ought to be followed while devising a social event. It is thought to be better and more effective when the purposes are defined and separated for the events.

For events that are basically planned for employee enjoyment, the suggested precautions are:

- The HR department should not officially plan or organize the event. These nonbusiness functions can be charted out by social committees or similar groups.
- The HR department should make sure that the company is not named as the sponsor of the event. Various methods of advertising can be thought of in the likes of signs, fliers, or posters to promote the event.
- The volunteer committees should be responsible for all aspects of the event's promotion.
- There must not be any compulsion for employees to participate. That is, employee participation must not be made mandatory. The moment socializing becomes compulsory, it becomes another everyday routine, the comfort level decreases and the easygoing factor flies out the window. Rather, a relaxed attitude automatically encourages employee participation.
- If employees incur certain expenses during the course of the organizing the event, the HR department must reimburse the

expenses incurred. This further relaxes employees, and the event will have an extra soothing effect.

- The teams participating in the event ought to be sponsored. This not only is a promotional factor but also acts in enhancing the self-confidence of the employee to a great extent. She views it as a token of appreciation for her ability. This satisfaction inevitably reflects positively on the productivity level of the company.

- Even in the remote sense of use, HR should not state or imply that the attendance at the event will foster an improvement in the employee's position in the company. Neither should HR hint that this attendance could be a potential topic during the evaluation of the employee's performance.

- The HR department must not promote the event as an annual custom or use any similar terms that can indicate company ownership in the event. If the name of the company is featured even in the remotest of terms, it will be inferred that the company is the sponsor of the event.

All the above guidelines will make it distinctly clear to employees that the event or function is organized with sole motive of promoting socializing.

TIPS FOR THE SOCIALIZING EXPERT:

Here are some tips for the benefit of the HR manager, who can effectively use them to promote work relationships and team spirit within the organization.

Allow a Certain Degree of Flexibility in Work Schedules

This of course, should be implemented with respect to the feasibility quotient. A lot of experts in the field of human capital have suggested that flexi-timing can be introduced as a sort of reward for a certain achievement. It can be a free reward for the company and potentially offers the most gain with the least pain.

For example, flexi-timing can be offered in the form of temporarily altered work schedules. This can provide time for family on important or emergency occasions or for personal issues like doctor's appointments or running a banking errand.

The HR department needs to know that the concerned employee really deserves the benefit and does not have any intention of abusing the privilege offered to her. This trend of flexi-timing can go a long way toward building trust and cultivating mature relationship with responsible and competent employees.

Write and Send Handwritten Notes

When the HR manager writes a personal handwritten note to an employee who deserves recognition, it is a huge positive acknowledgment for the recipient of the note. It acts as a great confidence booster too. This is a form of employee recognition that can work wonders to promoting the productivity of the organization.

Make Work Fun

When followed continuously, routine and regulations are sure to bring in monotony, and boredom can sound the death knell for enthusiasm in a work culture. So a bit of fun and relaxation that does not go against the company policies culture is always welcome. Change is not merely relaxing; it also sharpens the intellect and enhances attention and retention levels.

Here is an interesting example of something that I personally did to boost morale and introduce fun in the workplace:

In one of the companies I used to work for, I found that the employee morale of a certain segment of the organization was way below the desired level. No amount of energizing pep talks did any good for the situation. I suggested that, for one Sunday morning, every employee bring a picture of herself as a baby into the office and post it on a wall. Then the employees were asked to match their coworkers with the right picture.

The exercise turned out to be a lot of fun. It was as if the child in each of them came out, gurgling with laughter. And the result of the effort? The productivity level of the employees shot up to 70 percent from a meager 50 percent in the course of a single week.

Help Employees Connect

The two primary goals of socializing are to build a working circle and to network effectively. Accordingly, HR can begin by introducing employees to the key suppliers of the company, the customers, and a few members of senior management who can either make or improve the employees' careers. This helps the development of the team and fosters good relationships in different departments of the organization. What's more—it does not cost a single dollar for the company.

Loosen the Shoes

The HR professional can take this literally or metaphorically. One of my friends is an HR manager who suggested implementing a no-shoes policy, because she wanted to make employees feel at home in the office.

The feeling of comfort that is built translates into increased productivity. What she actually said was, "It's great to be in an office where employees are more concerned about doing quality work than what shoes or jewelry they have on. We get so much done."

Metaphorically, the situation can be suggestive of an environment of relaxation in which employees can let their guards down. They are allowed to be themselves and not constantly work under the hard cover of stiff formalities. It induces comfort and reduces work pressure.

Send Employees to Showers

The occasions of births, weddings, and anniversaries all deserve a "shower." These could become parties which all the employees attend. Employees may be allowed to leave early on such days, which allows employees to relax and return to work the next day with fresh minds.

Reward Not Only Success But Effort

Success cannot be guaranteed without effort behind it. The wholehearted effort is manifested in success, which is there for everyone to see. It gets easily acknowledged and instant recognition. But there are often cases in which an honest effort does not get effective results. If the considerate HR manager makes a point of evaluating the effort and likewise recognizes the basis of its earnestness, it serves as an effective confidence and morale booster for the individual.

The company can never meet success without effort and ideas. So even if the idea fails, the organization always needs it to be produced. So it does make sense to positively recognize those employees. There can be something like an award for "the best idea that did not work" at the annual staff forum of the company.

Give Employees a Free Pass

The HR department can offer a certain number of off days to employees that they will be free to use in any way they wish. When employees are given a few such free days in a year, they do not need to pretend sickness or offer desperate excuses to get leave.

Without any guilt or fear, they can go shopping, play with their children, or even visit a spa. They will not be accountable to the company for that time. As a result, employees will believe the HR team to be very considerate, and their sense of gratitude and satisfaction will translate into increased productivity levels.

Dole Out Cream and Sugar

This is actually a very basic idea to improve employee relations. During the busiest season of work, the company can provide drinks and refreshments for employees. In the hectic situation, they will appreciate it. The significance here lies in how well small gestures can build great companies. Once employees feel that their needs are taken care of, they will quite happily put in their best efforts for the development of the organization.

Just Blow Out the Candles

The HR team should not be an inhabitant of the locker room. While working with human capital, the HR professional needs to understand the sentiments of the people she works with. She gets to know their expectations and develops a clearer picture of what the employees are supposed to do.

It can be a luncheon with an employee whose birthday is in that particular month. There can also be a session in which employees are invited to ask HR professionals anything they want. This practice makes the employees feel recognized, and they become more comfortable sharing their ideas and opinions with their supervisors. The HR team stands to gain their loyal support and honest opinions.

Spread the Love

HR could institute a practice in which employees write down a quality they truly like or admire about one of their coworkers and frame it along with a photograph of the employee it's about. This can then be put on the wall. This helps healthy feelings get across and cultivates strong relationships over time. This is a sound method of effective management in the organization.

Offer a Swap

A swap gives an employee the chance to pick and choose her projects or trade tasks with her coworker. This is granted as a reward to the best and competent employees. This practice has a two-pronged function, uniquely empowering and rewarding the employee at the same time. She feels recognized and valued.

Applaud the Efforts of Employees

The HR manager is the guiding force for employees. She is the one to whom they look for direction. Her style of management is viewed as the ideal work system, so they naturally look to her for recognition and appreciation. To be an expert socializer, the HR manager ought to possess natural warmth, which should be reflected in her attitude.

The achievements and sincere efforts of the employees should be applauded, literally and sincerely. If something truly worthwhile has been accomplished by an employee, the HR department can organize something simple like a standing ovation from the entire staff in the next general meeting. It is perceived as a huge act of acknowledgment by the concerned individual. It not only builds confidence but also significantly boosts morale.

Say It with Flowers

Every style of acknowledgment has its own psychological connotations. Greeting an employee with flowers is also a confidence-boosting acknowledgment for an employee who has achieved a goal.

The greeting style could be something like the flower, which is a token of acknowledgment, being placed on the desk of the employee in the morning. That way it will be clear to every employee what the flower means. This method has actually been practiced in a few organizations, and the results were truly surprising. Even the commonly perceived cynical male attitude gave way, and the men fiercely competed to obtain the flowers. Such is the impact of honest acknowledgment.

"Pass the bucks"

A custom can be introduced into the organization in which an employee who has done something outstanding or accomplished something unusual can be presented with token Monopoly money. HR can call them anything—redemption coupons or "wow! Bucks"—and they can be extraordinary expressions of acknowledgment.

These bucks need not be strictly free. HR can provide an option such that they can be redeemed for gifts and other goodies. That means that they can eventually be traded for real goods and that is satisfying for the employee.

There is little doubt that they pay off handsomely in the long course. Such methods of acknowledgment and encouragement have been observed to hugely enhance employee performance at every level.

Share Memories

The HR leader could hold regular conversation sessions with her employees during which she could not only speak to them in a comfortable atmosphere to share her memories and experiences with them. This can prove to be a comfort-level enhancer and a learning opportunity for employees.

The HR leader could share her experiences from what she had done as an employee in a previous organization in a given situation—this, of course, must be relevant to the situation her employees are in. She can talk about the impact it had on the company and her coworkers.

The whole thing might seem to be a boasting session but should be done with such a friendly manner that it is engaging and sounds interesting. If done appropriately, her employees will look forward to the session each month.

A friend of mine, who is a senior and extremely successful HR professional, received a very touching gift at the end of his twenty-year HR career. The gift was a scrapbook created by his employees, chronicling various incidents that had occurred over the course of his career and had had an indelible impact on the organization and its employees alike. People who had worked with him wrote testimonials about his effective and unassuming leadership.

In fact, through such memory sharing sessions, an influential leader can carefully provide insight into important matters or relevant policies that may not have gone down well with employees. She can also deal with a lot of sensitive issues.

The employees not only receive clues but also significant directives given in a subtle manner as the HR leader relates her experiences.

Set Up Something Like the Wall of Fame

This is actually along the lines of a Hall of Fame for achievers. This wall can be set up in a prominent place in a public space inside the organization, or on the company's intranet. Employees who have accomplished something truly special have their photographs placed on the wall along with details of their achievements.

HR will see a stampede among workers to give their best in order to earn a place on the wall. It would be a matter of esteem apart from also being a gesture of acknowledgment.

Create a Club

This club is not along the lines of a regular club. It will have a different appeal, enabling the employees to relax completely. Different innovative ideas can be brought into play. This club can be set up in an unused office area, and it should be a quiet area that exudes calmness.

Employees could do a lot of things in the area; they could meditate, take a quiet nap, chill out, or even re-center themselves. In short, the place should make them feel refreshed, recharged, and ready to resume their duties. In fact, this in fact could be a ground-breaking idea that would make the company a great place to work. The employees will benefit and also feel cared for.

Stoke Their Passion

If an HR professional wants the best from her employees, she should not treat them like mercenaries. They are not a set of robots that will complete their tasks no matter what. They need to feel their work is significant and enjoy doing it.

People give their best when they are passionate about their work. So it is the duty of the HR leader to ignite their passion. She needs to enable employees to enjoy their work, and they will automatically feel passionate about it.

For this, the HR professional must ensure that her employees feel valued. She needs to inspire them to become passionate about their work by leading from the front. Employees tend to take directives and guidance from the HR leader, so she ought to be consciously perfect in her attitude.

She must already have a work system handy that will mould, control, and direct the implementation of ideas. With its help, the HR leader can encourage her employees to make their own decisions on certain issues while remaining confident in the outcome.

The HR leader should take care not to compromise the enthusiasm, the creativity, and—above all—the hard work that ensures the effectiveness of the work culture. Such a practice would help employees to learn and be a proactive and productive part of the system.

Reward Employees with a Good Place to Park

This can be a nice way to express acknowledgment for an achievement. The employee receives the opportunity to park her car in the best parking spot. The place would be reserved for a month or so for an employee who has done something truly worthwhile.

It would be even better if the spot could be just next to the CEO's Lexus. The employee might then have a chance to chat with her on her way in from the car. That way the parking opportunity can serve not only as a desired reward but also as an important opportunity to gain recognition from corporate management.

Remember the Spouses

This can be a good way to build healthy employee relationships with the HR department. The HR leader need not memorize the details of his employees' spouses. The employees are primarily committed to the organization, but it is not the sole definition of their existence.

The point I am trying to make is that the HR professional must recognize that her employees are not solitary beings, they belong to their families and are committed to them.

One of my friends happened to be a successful HR professional and had the following experience. An important delegation was to arrive for an immediate strategic partnership with my friend's company, and the date of arrival decided on was a Saturday. The entire staff had to be present for the occasion, so the employees had to devote their Saturday to the company.

The next morning, my friend, the HR manager, bought a bouquet of roses for each of his employees. He handed one to each employee with a note apologizing to her spouse for detaining her from her family on a weekend. The following day he received thank you notes from each of the spouses with one exception—one of his employee's spouses sent a letter saying that he was welcome to keep his spouse in office every weekend!

By acknowledging the employees' families, the HR leader can establish a healthy relationship with her employees. She can easily personalize the environment to make it more comfortable and fun to be in it. She can have a tremendously positive psychological impact on her employees. The result: a better work environment coupled with high productivity.

Let an Employee Phone In

Providing telecommuting programs once in a while relieves stress and makes your employees feel more appreciated and more productive. The HR manager can reward a deserving employee by awarding her with a single day of telecommuting and then add additional days according to performance.

Practices in the modern corporate world suggest that the flexibility to collect and drop off the kids for football practice, make a relaxing visit to the spa during the afternoon, or cut out early to avoid traffic congestion are highly popular. Such practices are gaining wide acceptance and appreciation for being unusually effective performance enhancers.

Employees consider these options more attractive and beneficial than slogging for sixty hours a week to obtain a fatter paycheck.

Remember the Two Secret and Sacred Words

Recent studies have revealed that the two most underused words in the modern corporate world are "Thank You." The HR professional is expected to be a human capital expert, so she ought to know better that these two words have the potential for the highest return on investment (ROI) and return on time (ROT).

The HR leader should learn to use them frequently and say them like she really means it rather than mumble it like an automated machine. The HR professional should make it a point to tell an employee what she specifically liked and not leave it to the employee's imagination. The earnestness in her tone will be perceived as a positive gesture for work well-done and act as a morale booster.

Socialize

Socializing should be spontaneous and not be reduced to a monotonous routine. No one is interested in that kind of celebration, and it does not enhance HR's credibility or effectiveness. The importance and necessity of socializing is to make the work environment comfortable. Socializing enables employees to feel like a natural part of the organization and increase productivity. Therefore, any attempt on this account ought to be done earnestly and be combined with a healthy dose of emotion.

If the HR leader fails to maintain a minimum standard of socializing with her employees, she might suffer the humiliation of employee noncooperation. They listen to her instructions and give the minimum effort to get the job done. They are not passionate about their work and act like they are doing her a great favor simply by doing their duties. They don't carry on any conversation beyond the purview of the relevant work.

The HR leader may consider herself very capable but be left frustrated by the behavior of her employees. Production levels will remain stagnant and the work atmosphere has no charm and enthusiasm in it.

In such a case, an HR professional felt it was time to obtain expert advice. The cause that emerged was that because the HR leader continuously refused her coworkers' invitations for lunch, happy hours, and other social gatherings, she was considered to be either a monstrous snob or socially handicapped.

The fact was that the HR professional felt that the employees may have invited her out of compulsion, and they might not feel comfortable in her presence; the invitation was not genuine. Nothing could be more absurd than this notion.

As an HR professional, she had been propagating the importance of each worker to feel like part of the organization, but being their senior, she did not present herself as part of her employees. The manner in which the HR leader gets along with the associates in her office has a huge impact on the work environment.

Schmooze with Employees

This is essential to foster a healthy and comfortable work atmosphere. If coworkers feel snubbed, it will, in the course of time, taint their professional relationship with the HR professional.

It is advisable to accept a couple of after-work invitations every month. It will be a good effort to socialize. The HR professional gets the opportunity to know the coworkers outside the work environment, which will enable her to build good personal relationships that will have positive impacts on productivity levels.

Here are a few options that can directly help with positive socializing with employees:

Charity Events

The majority of large and reputable companies organize their own charity events. If the company does not sponsor any charity events, the HR leader can generate her own ideas or identify the interests of the majority of her employees. Seek out a charitable cause and ask for the presence, participation, and cooperation of the employees of the organization.

Not only is it a good social cause, but it enables everyone in the office to stand and work on a level platform for a selfless cause. It is a great way to improve professional and personal relationships. Further, the HR leader also gets an opportunity to test the organizational skills of employees.

Sport Teams

Being a part of and building one's own sports teams provide good publicity exercises for the corporate world. It is a great way to blow off steam from work and also give the HR leader the chance to spend fun time with employees.

The most popular sports that big companies have teams for are football, bowling, golf, and basketball. Such activities promote good health and foster team spirit. There is also the option of organizing a game night for fun and enjoyment.

Business Carpools

Another effective way to promote socializing is through carpooling, which is a wonderful way to protect the environment. The HR manager can build a company- or department-wide list to denote who lives near where. Like that, carpools can be organized and the HR manager should be part of it. This promotes personal relationships in a brilliant way.

The ultimate goal of the HR leader is to be known and trusted by employees and help increase productivity. To achieve this, HR professionals are required to build relationships with their workforces. To do that, they ought to be visible—walk through the hallways, attend meetings, and chat with people.

Whatever the work culture in the organization, the HR leader can effectively build trust through socializing. The extremely positive impact of socializing can be such that the entire workforce seems like a happy family. Lunch, drinks, coffee, or picnics all happen together.

Honesty originates from trust. When employees trust the HR leader and her department, they will be more willing to share their concerns. Through comfortable conversation, the HR professional will come to know the actual reason behind low morale in the workforce, behind a feeling of discontentment over a particular policy, or behind any other problem that might be current. She will be more competently able to handle and improve the work environment.

In fact, socializing allows the HR leader to feel the climate of her organization through watercooler gossip and gauge problems that need to be addressed immediately. Actually, socializing involves a little bit of subtle private investigation, too.

An HR professional who is a socializing expert can mould and control the work environment according to the regulations and requirements of the company. She can train her workforce and issue directives in an acceptable manner for her employees. She ensures performance and allegiance to the organization by enhancing employees' comfort levels through personalization. Therefore, the principle achievement of this extensive exercise is that egos are under control and do not stand the risk of being bruised at the slightest provocation.

But the problems an HR leader might face while socializing include the following situations. Say the HR leader is in a compassionate or empathizing conversation with her employees who are discussing a concern with her. Very soon, the talk turns into gossip. The HR professional should be wary of such conversations; she cannot be a part of any gossip as it will only endanger her credibility.

Even in an atmosphere of congenial comfort, employees expect the utmost professionalism from the HR leader. She should take care to demonstrate it.

Consider the next situation. The HR leader is talking about a certain company policy that did not go down well with employees. She relays to an employee what talks transpired between her and senior management on the issue. While relating the facts, she must be very careful of the connotations that she might be expressing unconsciously. No negative comments about the company's inner workings should slip out. She should not say anything like, "I tried to justify your point of view, but the CEO doesn't give a damn about your concerns." Rather, if this is the case, she should relate the conversation in a manner closer to: "We had a lengthy discussion about the issue, and we are still working on it. Hopefully you will know the outcome soon."

Employees easily understand management jargon, and she will be saved from negative apprehensions about her credibility, trust, and sense of consideration for her employees. An effective HR strategy always calls for a neutral standing and for carrying on with the job with full integrity.

The HR professional must always be careful about the possible perceptions that her employees have of her words and actions. Say there is a possible job opening; the HR leader should not blast off the lid with all of the information in an effort to bond with an employee. She should follow the adage, "think twice before opening your mouth." She must wait until the vacancy is officially posted. Otherwise, it may look like the HR professional favors a particular employee because she fed her unofficial information, discriminating against others.

Such situations can result in irreparable damage to the credibility of the HR department.

Some complications can emerge if an HR professional becomes friends with one of her. Other workers fear undue discrimination and unjustified favoritism on the part of the HR leader. The particular employee who is friends with the HR professional has to bear suspicions of being a conniver who exercises undue and unfair influence.

Basically, the HR professional must maintain the impartiality of the work environment even if a personal relationship exists. Being friends at work is certainly not against the rules. One cannot deliberately avoid it, but life in office is surely easier without that relationship.

Actually, the HR leader must be overtly cautious while being congenial, but at the same time, she must not appear standoffish. It is better to be friendly than to be friends. She needs to maintain her open and approachable attitude. Any perception of favoritism can undermine the leader's or department's objectivity.

Still, it would be an overreaction to say that the HR leader cannot make friends at work. She can develop friendships just like anyone else, but she needs to have boundaries for those friendships. We do it all the time outside of work. You can be very good friends with someone, but you may not ask her how much money she makes. You consciously maintain this boundary because it is none of your business. The same principles can be applied to work friendships too. Stay away from delivering and obtaining confidential information.

There is another danger that the HR professionals might face during a socializing session: inappropriate questions. After all, HR does deal with gossip-friendly things that everyone likes to talk about—that is, about someone who is leaving or is sacked or about someone who is being promoted or disciplined. Therefore, in a situation when an employee asks the HR leader something inappropriate, she should decline politely but firmly from discussing it. Employees automatically understand that certain information cannot be accessed.

In a situation in which a friend of the HR leader stands for promotion but does not get it, that leader would naturally think of helping her friend. But that can set tongues wagging in the workforce. When the friend needs to be either disciplined or laid off, the HR leader is again in a fix. Things can get unduly tough when it means hurting or potentially losing a friendship. The HR professional cannot afford to let friendship get in the way of her job. The moment she realizes that she is under the influence of a friendship, she should remove herself from the decision-making. In fact, this sense of idealism in the HR professional offers her the high pedestal of nobility, and this is what is most appealing in the profession. Objectivity and integrity in her responsibilities and her profession is the supreme concern in the life of the HR professional.

There are specific characteristics of the HR leader who is naturally a good socializer. Her attitude reflects two specific aspects of her personality: she has a natural desire to build relationships and is always direct in her dealings. This means that she has an aggressive approach and is fast-paced in her actions. The employees consider the socializing HR leader to be a bit playful, approachable, and fun to work with. Beyond work, she does not spend time in solitude, and her general interest lies in interacting with her employees. The socializing HR leader is adept at making easy conversation and thus talks a lot. She is extremely cooperative and capable of building good teams. She is an excellent organizer and gets her job done pretty quickly. She acts mostly on intuition. She arrives at her decisions quickly. Since she is approachable and easygoing, employees find it easy to communicate with her.

There is one thing that people need to be careful of while dealing with this type of HR professional—they tend to be very concerned about their personal prestige and they are quite sensitive about their acceptance.

Socializing has become an essential ingredient of a successful HR life. Attending and being an active part of management functions and events is a necessity for a person in a management position. These events are basically viewed as an extension of work. If the HR leader fails to show up for a recognition dinner or refuses to be part of the company picnic, she is telling her senior management and employees that they are of no importance to her. After all, the reason companies sponsor such events is to bring all employees together to create a more caring, family-style atmosphere.

Two things that the HR professional must do while socializing:
She Should Work the Crowd
Parties, functions, and events are an opportunity to meet people from all levels. The HR professional ought to make good use of this opportunity to roam around and conduct positive, productive conversations with all of her employees. She should avoid staying with a particular group.

She Should Take the Initiative to Make Introductions
The HR leader should introduce new recruits to the other employees, as well as introducing people from other departments to each other as they would otherwise never meet in the course of their work. She could also sensibly guide their conversations in a manner that they get to know more about each other and become acquainted with each other's talents and interests. This will build a healthier work environment.

SOCIALIZING INVOLVES GATHERING INFORMATION FIRST-HAND
The HR function depends on fast and easy access to accurate information, which is primarily obtained through socializing. It is necessary for structuring, updating, enforcing or tracking existent policies. It is also required to keep employees up-to-date on matters relevant to them.

The HR professional gets to know about the prevalent work environment and the levels of satisfaction. Then, it is easier to understand any requirement for specific disciplinary measures or any discontentment brewing.

The HR professional should have instant access to information obtained on a first-hand basis. This means that the information can be obtained by the HR leader while socializing with her employees. That is the reason why socializing is a bit of private investigation.

She is required to have complete and unqualified, access-controlled visibility to company-wide information. This follows from secure collaboration with her employees but within the guidelines of ethical management.

In the business context of obtaining relevant information, the HR professional transform seemingly incongruent pieces of information into a concise web of company-specific knowledge. If done appropriately, the operations of the HR department will be at the most efficient level.

First-hand information can be obtained through:
Visibility
The HR leader must practice and maintain something called "information transparency" in the organization. Apart from receiving information verbally, she should receive documents, spreadsheets, and e-mails that are easily and instantly retrievable.

Secure Collaboration

Since the HR team works in secure project spaces, project-specific information is available team-wide with just a click of the mouse. The HR professional should be careful while sharing relevant files, updating information, and tracking activity in the workplace. The information that she gathers during this process can go a long way toward framing future policies and strategies related to the success of the project.

E-mail Management

The HR leader should have a good e-mail management system in which the mails can be automatically filed and organized. This makes them instantly accessible. She is not dependent on others, and there is no missing information and no frustration.

Seamless Integration

The HR professional should be well-aware of and well-practiced with her resources on this account. Information is the most precious thing that HR deals with. For the effective management of human capital, information must be integrated in the existing management system. She must know what she has and how she can put them to the best possible use.

The most important point that needs to be stressed here is that this entire range of information must be gathered-first hand. The HR leader must have direct access to her individual sources of information. She must be careful not to receive any information via a separate source. Otherwise, there is a chance of the information getting manipulated and distorted, which could cause serious problems for the HR professional and the company.

Say that, while obtaining information about a particular employee's professional details, work schedule, and other such matters, the HR professional should limit her queries to the relevant employee. If the HR professional happens to obtain information from any coworker of the employee, she would voluntarily give rise to the possibility of gossip and backbiting. This can do immense damage to the work environment.

The nature of the information that the HR leader receives through socializing commonly pertains to employment discrimination and retaliation. As such, the HR professional is required to take appropriate measures that are based on legitimate work-related criteria. That should applicable to every stage of the employment relationship from recruiting through termination.

The HR leader should also be prepared to be at the receiving end of allegations by an employee that a member of the company has dishonored one or more of the employment discrimination laws. Such an allegation can have a serious effect on the organization. The principle result will be a tarnished reputation for the HR leader and her department. Good employees may leave their jobs. The company stands to lose its clients or customers and money and other resources will need to be spent on the attorneys needed to defend against those allegations. The net result would be an unhealthy work atmosphere and a negative productivity quotient. In such a situation, it does not matter whether the HR leader regrets not exercising enough caution while obtaining or handling the information because the damage is already done, and the results are serious.

Effectiveness in dealing with information can be enhanced by cultivating a well-organized HR department. Organization would reap a successful and satisfied workplace. Though the task might seem overwhelming, an innovative human resource management system can prove to be just what the doctor ordered; it can provide the best environment for the business to develop and flourish. The system mentioned above is a document storage system that consolidates information on the processes of recruiting, training, and administering benefits to improve HR efficiency. It is a centralized, integrated, and cost-effective solution. With its aid, the HR department can become a highly efficient and responsive department that benefits its employees, organization, and the social environment at large.

It can also be concluded that being a fun-loving, sociable HR professional is not enough, as she also needs to have proper access to relevant information and is capable of using it to the advantage of the organization.

Chapter 7

HR Manager: the Great Recruiter

Distinguishing the Great Employee from the Good Employee

The human resource manager's success depends on how she navigates between the requirements of management and the needs of employees. It is important to build strong relationships between the clients/customers and the employees of the organization. For that, the HR professional needs good recruitment understanding, technique, and ideology. She must ensure that each employee understands her importance to the success of the company.

Proper orientation and training of new employees undoubtedly pays off in the form of retention, superior productivity, and customer satisfaction. The process of hiring, acquainting new recruits to other employees, and accustoming the new recruits to the work environment is known as on boarding. This refers to everything the HR manager does to enable a new employee to feel confident about good performance. On boarding is an extremely important process because the HR professional cannot expect the new employee to perform well unless she feels integrated as a part of the team.

SO HOW IS IT DONE?

Set Out the Welcome Mat

First, HR should introduce the new employee to her immediate supervisor. HR should not just end the introduction with names but strike up an easy conversation and personalize the process. The HR professional should help the new employee to relax. One option for accomplishing this could be a welcome lunch or a social function, which will help a new recruit feel comfortable.

Second, the HR department could place a welcome notice addressing the new employee on a bulletin board or the company's intranet. The notice should include the name, photograph, and designation particulars for the new employee. It should include a collection of similar photos of the current staff along with title and name. This will help everyone remember who is who. When the HR department posts photos from company events, it enhances camaraderie and helps new employees to explore, while at the same time feeling like part of the company culture.

The Approach Should Be Simple

Proper implementation of the above on boarding procedures results in a massive reduction of employee turnover, because the HR department saves both time and money without needing to retain a struggling worker. Particularly since a worker would seldom struggle, if she struggles at all. Therefore training employees as soon as they join the organization is profitable in more than one way.

What Should Be the Desired Methodology?

The HR manager's style of employee orientation should focus on the larger picture. She cannot possibly expect someone who has just been hired to remember the operational details of every department. The HR professional should not simply race forward—speed breakers are necessary for a smooth ride. Successful training should always be patient and steady and allow the new employee to absorb what they are being taught while the HR professional also has time to focus on keeping pace with the functions of the company.

This could be done efficiently by writing introductory material that includes the company's history, a general overview of the company's product and services, and the rules, regulations, and policies for all employees. This orientation material must be precise, straightforward, and free of ambiguity. It should be simple and, at the same time, interesting. It should also be composed in a motivational style, which will be readily visible when the employee receives it the first day.

The final step to the process includes giving proper direction to the in-house trainers, familiarizing the new employee with the entire operation of the company while honing her skills and, in the process, shaping up as perfect recruits.

This on boarding process is just the beginning of the employee procedure that constitutes the responsibility of the HR manager. She therefore needs to strategize constantly to bring things in line with the requirements of the company. She should plan for upcoming staffing needs and define the career paths of excellent employees.

The sole point that should never be forgotten in this entire on boarding process is that the personalized approach must never lose its sheen. It is the prime responsibility of the HR manager to make the new employee feel comfortable and suitably motivated.

I.   Recruitment and Selection of Employees

First, the HR department needs to undertake an analytical study of the job in question. The essential factors that will determine the effective performance of that job need to be identified and sorted out. This should be jotted down in a job description. It enables the recruiter and the selection department to be clear about what they are actually looking for in a recruit. The description should include the physical and the mental characteristics of the employee and the desired qualities and attitude. It will likewise identify the characteristics that would be a decided disadvantage in the position.

In the case of replacing staff, HR needs to decide if recruitment is needed for that position, because for an efficient HR department, replacement is rarely an automatic process.

Recruiting an employee is alternately referred to as buying an employee—the decided price being the wage or salary multiplied by probable years of service. Therefore, a good calculative and rational reasoning is needed for an effective and profitable deal. A bad recruitment can incur loss for the company and damage to the HR leader's reputation. The HR manager has the option of obtaining the services of external expert consultants for a reliable opinion. They aid in the recruitment and selection process.

II. What Are the Possible Avenues of the Recruiter?

- advertising—this includes agents for specialist posts and can be done through the use of the local print or electronic media.
- university appointment boards;
- recruitment agencies;
- career fairs;
- employee referral programs; and
- internal transfers or promotions—this is a very desirable avenue as the security of the company morale is upheld.

The organization can have its own advertising process for the print and electronic medium, or it can employ the services of another company. HR must be careful to include an identifying logo as its original trademark. The advertisement should in no way offend the gender, age, religion, or any sort of minority either intentionally or unintentionally.

The form documenting the personal appearance, letter of application, and completion of a form will vary according to the designated posts. This is particularly desirable for those jobs in which the column of experience and statements include health. The HR department needs to keep an eye on the claims and statements about these qualifications

If required, HR should organize a medical examination. Before letters of appointment are issued to newcomers, any doubts regarding medical fitness or capacity with respect to the job requirements must be allayed. Any hygiene consideration should also be a prominent feature of this process. The fears and concern of the company ought to be understood by the new employees. Again, this is the job of the successful recruiter.

The interview process can be conducted by individuals like the supervisor, the departmental manager, or a panel of interviewers. The recruitment process can also consist of sequential interviews with different experts that vary from informal chats to a process involving several days. The basic idea should be a near-perfect, all-around screening of the applicant. The judgment skill of the successful recruiter comes into play here.

A tiny dosage of training while interviewing will test the candidate suitably and, to a great extent, allow the expert HR manager to fulfill her task. The strategy of the HR manager consists of teaching and explaining the interviewers how to draw out the interviewee while helping the interviewee relax. The rating that is established consists of evaluating the new recruits on the basis of experience, knowledge, physical/mental capabilities, intellectual levels, motivation, prospective potential, and leadership abilities, among a host of other things. Needless to say, all of these ought to conform to the requirements of the particular position and to the company's competency framework. The HR manager's adherence to this normal curve of distribution for scoring or evaluation will surely eliminate the possibility of poor judgments.

III. The HR Department's Formulation of the Recruitment Process:

- The HR manager needs to nominate the selection committee members.
- She needs to decide and confirm the committee meeting and the interview schedule.
- She needs to ensure the observation of the company's recruitment and selection policy.
- She needs to make the understanding of the position and requirements of the prospective candidate clear to the committee members.
- The short-listing of the written applications needs to be compiled.
- She needs to decide on the selection techniques.
- She needs to formulate the interview questions.
- She needs to establish contact with the candidate to schedule the interview. The selection committee members must also be informed if any specific selection technique is to be used.
- She needs to oversee the interview procedure.
- She needs to check the references, if any.
- She needs to complete the selection committee report.

IV. The Formation of the Selection Committee

The committee is required to assess and select the candidate. The HR manager arranges all the selection committee activities.

The formation process includes:

1. **Nominating the Committee Members**—The selection committee must have at least three members. However, the number depends on the type and level of the recruitment position. All the committee needs to promote is efficient

and effective decision-making, which is ensured by adequate representation—this guarantees the best and fairest decision.

- The committee must include individuals who have expertise in the area of the appointment.
- The committee must reflect the direct reporting relationship of the position concerned.
- The committee must include someone who does not belong to the unit to provide a broader view of the process.
- The committee must include members from diverse backgrounds.
- Whenever possible, the committee must reflect gender balance.

The members of the selection committee have the responsibility to observe the confidentiality and to respect the privacy of the candidates.

2. **Confirming the Meeting and Interview Times**

    The schedule must be agreed to.

    - Discuss the position and shortlist the written applications.
    - Choose the selection techniques.
    - Decide on the interview questions to ask.
    - Interview the candidates.

V.   Short-Listing the Candidates

Short-listing involves three major steps:

Discussing the Position

Usually, it is the responsibility of the HR department to do the short-listing; however, it is preferable to hold a meeting with the selection committee to short-list the probable candidates for the interview. During the discussion, the committee members ought to have a clear understanding of the position, the requirements for the candidates, and, of course, the related work environment. The company's recruitment and selection policy is a must-read.

The Making of the Shortlist

The submitted applications or the search firm profiles are assessed to short-list suitable candidates for interview. It is advisable to use a short-listing report Form.

The Submitted Written Application

The candidate's application ought to address the selection criteria. It should contain the details of the candidate's work experience, achievements, and qualifications. The committee should be able to judge the candidate's written communication skills and her analytical style of compiling, highlighting, and presenting information. This could act as an initial screening of the candidate.

The Search Firm Profiles

A search firm usually conducts a preliminary interview before providing a short-list for the organization to interview. The committee can then discuss the profile of each candidate from the provided information and then move on with the selection process.

Contact the Candidates

Contact is established with the short-listed candidates, and an interview date is arranged. The interview schedule should be set such that there is an hour for each interview and a fifteen minute-break between the interviews.

VI.   Choosing the Selection Technique

The selection technique is based on the requirements of the position—meaning, what the organization is looking for: a particular skill, attribute, or level of knowledge. It is always better to use varied selection methods. For example, work samples can be a great way to evaluate the candidate's capability. But they will not provide HR with an overview of how the candidate does daily. The interviewers know nothing about her typical performance. In one case, a candidate may be an excellent feature writer, but she writes only one great feature every one month!

DIFFERENT SELECTION TECHNIQUES:

- Structured Interview
- Telephone Interview
- Work Samples
- Peer Assessment
- Assessment Center
- Psychometric Profiling
- Informal Meeting

The interview questions are decided on as a team in the selection committee. First, they must decide on what constitutes an appropriate answer. The committee could present a specific work-related situation and evaluate the candidate's response. The HR department has the responsibility of administering the selection techniques, and then of following the interview guidelines and format.

INTERVIEW GUIDELINES

These guidelines will aid HR to hire a great employee instead of a good employee:

- Look at the length of time on each job in the candidate's resume. A candidate who has several short-term employers might lack commitment.
- Realize the need for explanation if there are gaps in the employment period. Long periods may infer possible service terminations.
- Verify that there are no overlaps in employment dates. Overlaps show that the candidate is not honest about previous employers.
- While reviewing resumes, have a copy of the job description close at hand. The more skills that match, the better the match.

The HR leader needs to guard against a few interviewing errors.

First, no judgment should be based on a superficial first impression. Potential coworkers and other team members can have an informal chat with the candidate about the post's requirements and share their opinions with the HR manager. References should be checked thoroughly. A grumpy first-day candidate may well become an adept public relations manager for the company.

Second, the HR manager should limit her talking. She ought to talk not more than 25 percent of the total interview time. Only then can she learn the maximum about the applicant.

Third, the HR manager should not rush to tell the applicant what she is seeking at the very beginning of the interview. She should remember that she is not the only smart person around. A skillful applicant might ask, "What kind of a person are you looking for to do this job?" The HR manager can provide a witty answer, like, "Someone like you, who welcomes a challenge."

Fourth, she should steer clear of hypothetical questions. A what if question can only provide her with theoretical answers. She would then be prone to misinterpret the candidate's answer to represent her ability to judge and perform. I have come across candidates who are good at theoretical what ifs but run for cover at the tiniest challenge in real life.

Fifth, the HR manager should not make the mistake of comparing candidates with each other. She should rather compare each one's past performance in relation to the present job's requirements. That will help her to stay focused on the great prospective employee.

Sixth, she should not search for her own clone! Just because both the HR manager and the candidate have similar interests—love football, agree on what's wrong with the world, graduated from the same university—does not mean that she'll be a replica of her genius self.

Seventh, the HR manager should not stereotype any candidate. One with curling tresses and soft delivery of speech is not necessarily the creative type. The interviewer should remember that a single trait cannot influence the other areas of performance.

Finally, she should not assume that the candidate already has certain past experiences that are similar to your own, which are necessary for success.

The HR manager should break the ice with an informal chat. She should follow this with open-ended questions to gather any missing information about preliminary requirements. After that, she should move to job-related questions. Following this session, she should tell the candidate a little about the job and the company. Finally, the HR manager let them know when she will be making the hiring decision.

If she has followed the above stated procedures, she is most likely in the process of hiring a great employee instead of a good employee.

It is always advisable to ask behavior-based questions during the interview. According to the conventionally structured interview format, the skills and attributes of the prospective employee are assessed through behavior-based questions. The interviewer can structure questions by citing a particular situation similar to what the candidate might face in the position for which she has applied. These questions ought to be styled in a manner that evokes specific responses about what the person has done in the past in similar circumstances. For example, she can ask something like, "Can you recollect or describe a situation in which,…" or "Can you tell me something about a time when…'

Behavioral questions enable the HR professional to evaluate the interviewees more objectively. She should receive precise answers to the conditions the company might offer the candidate, which will help her to think beyond personal impressions and those sticky gut feelings.

An important point needs to be made here: The HR professional must phrase her questions well. When she asks behavior-based questions, she should not even unconsciously ask for happy-ending success stories. Take this example in which the interviewer says, "Tell me about a time when you exceeded a customer's expectations." Both the high and low performers will answer this question pretty comfortably.

Improving the question pattern and style is fairly simple. The key is precision and logical phrasing. The HR professional should ask for actual and specific examples of past behavior that she wishes to hold as a reference point. She will find that the low performers exert the maximum effort offering diverse excuses as substitutes for a lack of results. Distinguishing between the comparative performance levels will become much easier.

It is also advisable to document the interview. The company may have its own documentation form on which the selection committee members can write the candidate's particulars and specific attributes in an organized manner. This may prove to be of immense help since its takes a considerable amount of time to arrive at a final decision. It is highly probable that minute but important facts might be forgotten during this period, so documentation comes in handy. It can also prove to be a good record for future interviews.

Recruiting is a time- and energy-consuming process. It requires an extensive design as it shapes the future of the company. No wonder an HR manager would like to ensure its success through her individual style of perfection, dynamism, and innovation.

CHAPTER 8

BUILDING THE COMPANY IMAGE

ESTABLISHING AND PROTECTING THE VALUES OF THE ORGANIZATION

The role and function of HR has undergone a dramatic change over the past decade. This transformation is the result of mounting global competition, aggressive technological advancement, and the persistent pressure to reduce operating costs. As a result, companies are undergoing both structural and cultural changes to remain successful, and the job is being done by none other than HR.

As companies disregard the old operating models, less emphasis is placed on HR processing and administration while more and more emphasis is placed on the strategic or value-added HR activities. HR has emerged as the builder of the company's image in the process.

Its critical role has become that of the organization's strategic business partner. HR must thus understand the business and the impact of the business decisions together with a good sense of the predictability of the outcome. HR professionals need to be experts in organizational change and development as well as possess state-of-the-art HR knowledge. They are responsible for organizational analysis, design and planning, change management, and leadership development.

The image of the organization is affected by several factors that force drastic changes in the organization. They include:

- an increasing trend toward more flat and agile management structures;

- reduced core functions;
- the impact of deregulation and liberalization; and
- increasing customer requirements.

As anyone can observe, all the above factors are everyday realities that require immediate attention and relevant action. The current HR system in the majority of organizations engages more of its time and resources on the administrative activities of the company, and in the process, strategic objectives get ignored.

The tasks that consume most of the HR leader's attention are:

- answering employee inquiries;
- solving employee problems;
- updating basic information;
- processing recruitment formalities;
- entering employee performance reviews;
- processing and distributing salary slips;
- arranging different training programs.

This immense effort spent on the administration of the company does not add much value to the organization. According to many studies, administration costs 60 percent of all human resources efforts but adds only 10 percent of the value. Service delivery takes 30 percent of HR efforts and provides 30 percent in added value. In comparison, HR strategic planning accounts for over 60 percent of the value added by the HR function while it costs only 10 percent in effort. What's more, it builds the company image.

THE NEW ROLE OF THE HR MANAGER

HR managers are required to develop their capabilities and deliver HR programs that successfully meet strategic business objectives. For this, they are expected to do the following.

- HR must reduce the cost of its services.
- HR must be able to identify the necessary skills and competencies to achieve the company's vision.
- HR must develop the proper programs to build those requisite competencies.
- HR must constantly be on its toes. The HR manager must react quickly to the continuous and rapid changes in business structures

- HR must develop innovative reward programs that can effectively attract new employees, provide motivation for current employees, and enable the retention of skilled and competent employees.
- HR must develop the necessary programs for the efficient and easy management of the overall performance of employees.
- HR must have a vision for the future, identifying and aiding in the development of competent performers so they can become future leaders.
- HR must be able to formulate new recommendations for HR structures and roles.

Such a style of HR role-playing brings about a considerable change in the organization's work environment and the manner in which the company discharges its functions. This has a direct impact on productivity and the company's customer relations. All the factors combined work to build the organization's image.

This has led to a visible change in the roles and expectations in which the human capital of the organization is managed.

- With employees feeling more valuable and important, their sense of responsibility increases. They are expected to take responsibility and thus ownership about their career development and overall progression.
- The company needs to increase the worth of its human capital, and the HR manager is expected to fulfill this requirement.
- The HR manager is entrusted with the maximum responsibility. She is supposed to provide the necessary equipment, processes, and programs to aid each employee to succeed in her role.

Therefore, the key roles that the HR structure takes on to build the company image are:

Strategic Partner. As a strategic partner, the HR leader focuses on aligning HR plans and practices with the business strategy of the company.

Improve Service Delivery. The existent HR processes are constantly under examination and being improved that gradually shifts in the direction of shared service and self-service.

Employee Champion. A successful and effective HR should persistently and aggressively develop the intellectual capital of the company and constantly associate the organization's success with the positive contribution of its employees.

Change Agent. The HR leader should understand and appreciate the critical processes of change. she ought to be committed to those processes and ensure that the change is manifested according to the devised plans.

The traditional corporate role of HR is undergoing massive transformation. The acquisition of new skills and better career structuring are necessary for HR professionals to remain marketable. This means that HR professionals need to reshape their roles to encompass a greater and more productive perspective than ever before. The suggestions given above are all essential and to help an HR professional to accept, embrace, and capitalize on the changes and challenges that arise in the course of her professional life.

The HR manager is expected to have a good understanding of people, hence the term *human resources*. Whether she is building or rebuilding the company image, she needs to focus on the five most essential steps that will ensure success.

Come Clean

The first thing that any HR manager needs to do is to remove confusion and ambiguity. Statements and directives issued by the HR department to employees must be crystal clear. No scope should be left for misapprehension or double meaning. HR needs to talk directly and clearly to the employees. If HR has any new plans or strategies in mind, they should update all employees the loop before actually enforcing the new changes or rules.

Conduct an Internal Employee Satisfaction Survey

A satisfaction survey can be a great way to initiate the building of the company image. It can act as a baseline to ascertain the current perceptions of the company in the industry. There is a ridiculous tendency to hold off on conducting this survey for fear of unfavorable factors being revealed. Delaying something like that is undoubtedly a costly mistake.

The survey actually provides HR and management with the opportunity to compare and contrast the company's situations and improvements, if any. Accomplishments and failures become clearer, and strategies become easier to devise. Moreover, these surveys are essential documents; they are concrete evidence for management to demonstrate whether a particular initiative from HR has worked or not. This enables the HR manager to get her point across with increased strength, more so, if the original decision did not enjoy the full support of senior management.

Bring in New Faces

This is the most objective way to build the company image. A quality team can be recruited or selected to stand in the forefront. The bad apples should be gotten rid of as soon as possible. When the existing employees find the new recruits taking charge with a positive attitude, the seasoned and the competent employees whose positivity or skill may be a bit dormant will find positive motivation for better performance. So that will be a double achievement for the expert called the HR manager!

Always Be Visible

The HR manager should ensure that anyone associated with the company—be it an employee or a customer or a client—should never wonder, "Who should I contact?" or "Who is going to answer this?" HR should always practice an open-door policy.

For this, she should be familiar with every face in her department and organization. The HR manager needs to make sure that she is visible and approachable for every employee. She must provide them with a high comfort level so they will confide in her, which will enable her to intercept potential problems and solve existing ones. As said in the previous chapter, a bit of socializing can be immensely effective. An occasional "cafeteria session" can be used to answer queries, address employee concerns, and even discuss HR or personnel policies.

With respect to customers or clients, a document that states who is responsible for overseeing which department and in what situation they should contact which department should be a readily available. In simple terms, a ready and functional helpline should always be available.

The above steps would work not only to improve the company's image but also to reestablish the efficiency and credibility and organizational skills of the HR leader and department. They would also allow executive management to be more confident as they running the company. How employees and customers think about the company is the bottom line. Therefore, it is the duty of the effective HR manager to promote a happy and productive company environment that translates into superior customer service.

In this discussion on how HR affects the company image, it's important to note that a few wrong choices can considerably tarnish the image as well. The following is the most common mistake that HR makes.

That mistake is bad or inappropriate hire. A bad hire can wreak massive damage on an organization if the new recruit makes a terrible decision or loses a great customer. In both circumstances, the company image suffers.

The following estimation is no exaggeration: The cost of a bad hire for the position of a software engineer can exceed 1 million dollars, and for a CEO it could reach more than a billion dollars.

Recruiting great people translates into great employees, and great employees make a great company. A company brand runs on human capital, so the equipment, other material, resources, and other forms of capital do not make the company run. It is actually the ideas and strategies of great brains that build the company image and reputation.

The following are the negative outcomes of hiring mediocre people:

- Mediocre employees require a good deal of management time and effort.
- They are high-maintenance liabilities who need increased management attention and are a cause of worry. As managers need to attend to more remedial training, their time-to-productivity ratio also slows down.
- Competent employees are deprived of time with management because that time is actually eaten up by mediocre employees.
- They have a definite multiplier effect on the productivity levels of the other employees.

Now what impact do they have on the company image?

- Mediocre employees possess a natural tendency to burden the company with extraordinary error rates. The ultimate result of their actions is borne by the customers.
- The existence of mediocre employees makes customers feel that the company is getting weak or that it no longer cares for them.
- Mediocre employees produce only mediocre ideas, and those ideas often prove to be a distraction from the company objective.

- Since they do not belong to the team of winners, mediocre ideas and performances have a negative impact on the market.
- To keep the team spirit unaffected and the work environment healthy, management has to be careful not to humiliate mediocre employees and waste valuable time and energy answering their questions. This would not be needed if they already understood.
- A mediocre employee sends a dangerous signal to the company's competitor that the organization is getting weak. It builds their confidence, and they emerge a bolder avatar in the industry.
- The production rate is lower per dollar of cost for a mediocre employee. As nearly 60 percent of a corporate budget is used to meet employee expenses, this inefficient use of funds results in massive corporate weakness. The impact is even more profound if the employee is an executive or a top manager. The adverse impact falls on the company's stock price.
- Future recruits of the company get a message that the employee selection strategy of the company is inadequate, and current employees may think that these new recruits are a sign that the company is heading downhill.
- The company also incurs disciplinary costs because of these mediocre employees; absenteeism and tardiness are regular habits for them.
- HR has to undertake the undesired load of more paperwork, more files, and HR holds to take the full responsibility for the hire. The trust, credibility, and competence of the HR department are questioned.

The image of the company is not solely dependent on its public relations (PR) mechanism. PR is responsible only as though providing the cover letter for a document. No doubt, the cover letter is important, but the contents need to be worthwhile too. And the contents are ensured by the HR department. Not only must that document be carefully put together and perfect in its dealing, but every mistake will be a negative mark on the company's ROI. And HR cannot afford to risk its reputation through negligence.

Chapter 9

How to Be a Lovable HR

Instill Your Belief in Employees and Function according to the Ethics of the HR Profession

HR plays a pivotal and important role in employee management and improvements in the organization's culture that lead to enhanced productivity. To be effective, HR needs to instill its own beliefs about the organization into employees, too. HR's commitment to the discipline and to its organization requires hard work done in an ethical fashion. Successful employee management in today's corporate world depends less on formal ethics programs and inclines more toward employees' perceptions of fairness, the ethical leadership in the HR structure, and a well-considered configuration of multiple formal and informal cultural systems that support ethical conduct. The HR manager must design leadership training to create and maintain an effective organizational culture of hard work and ethics.

The employees' perceptions of fairness are more important than other factors in the practice of ethics. If employees perceive unfair treatment, they tend to "balance the scales" by not preventing, or actively trying to, harm the organization. Employees who perceive fair treatment, on the other hand, will go above and beyond their call of duty to aid management and the entire organization.

To ensure this perception of fairness, it is important that the HR leader design systems and interventions with fairness as the prime objective. Any system should emphasize fair decision-making procedures and fair interpersonal treatment. Employees' perception of fair treatment must be regularly monitored through surveys, and changes should be made according to the results of the surveys. Acting on this fairness contributes to the effectiveness of an HR leader, while also making the whole office fond of the person. She becomes a lovable HR professional.

Generally, people think that *ethics* and *fairness* are synonymous. So, the majority of the concerns reported to HR are related to the HR system. There is no boundary between ethics and the HR office. There is no doubt that ethical leadership is a fundamental requirement of an ethical workforce. Most business leaders believe that employees are mature moral agents who are capable of leading themselves. However, the majority of employees tend to look beyond themselves to other significant sources for ethical guidance and direction. If the leadership of the company is unable to provide that guidance, confusion will proliferate.

So HR ethics calls for an ethical leader who truly listens to her employees. She should always be genuinely concerned about the employees' best interests. This ought to be complemented by a strong and regular communication of ethical values and messages. The first question to answer before making any decision should be, "What is the right thing to do here?"

The HR leader must transform into an ethical leader who can be a role model for ethical conduct. An ethical role model always gains the trust of her employees. She, therefore, must set an example of how to do things the right way to obtain effective results in terms of ethics. She ought to hold everyone, including herself, accountable. For her, success is defined not simply by results but by the manner in which it is achieved.

Along these lines, HR managers are required to design performance management, career development, and training programs, which should be characterized by holding the leaders accountable for the appropriate ethical dimension of their actions; identifying ethical leaders who can be made responsible for mentoring others; and incorporating the ethical dimension of leadership into every leadership and training program.

The prime focus of the HR department lies on performance management and rewards for employees. So the HR manager must devise strategies that value ethics. She should integrate performance management systems with accountability to ethics by assigning substantial weight to an individual's values in the course of promotion and compensation decisions.

Similarly, commendable ethical behavior should be rewarded by the HR or other managers. Likewise, discipline must be strictly maintained, and unethical conduct must be strongly disciplined so a powerful signal can be sent to the rest of the organization about how seriously the executive team regards ethics. Conducting regular assessments of the ethical culture in the work environment is also necessary; after all, the effectiveness of ethical conduct must be a common goal for employees and management alike.

The ethical code of conduct that the HR department must follow is broadly based on three fundamental principles:

Equity and Justice

This refers to universal fair treatment. Not a single employee or staff member should be discriminated against, ill-treated, or subjugated. Justice should be established on the basis of power sharing coupled with the prevention of the abuse of power. The work environment should allow every member to fully access every available opportunity.

Respect for People

The individuality of each employee must be respected. Everyone possesses the right to be honored and defended. This is, in fact, a psychological approach that builds a healthy environment and ensures good productivity. Respect empowers the employee to claim her rights and accomplish her optimum potential. Respecting the rights of every individual fosters community-building and development, because each employee begins to recognize and accept her corporate and social responsibilities, learning to behave with integrity. Once an employee acknowledges that she is a member of the larger community—that is, the organization—she not only starts to enjoy her rights but also accepts her duties and responsibility to act openly and honestly.

The HR professional is obliged to lead by example. She can demonstrate respect for a person's individuality during a case of a disagreement, during which arguments should be countered with reasonable arguments. Use of inappropriate style, tone, language, and words—suggesting racism or sexism—must be strictly avoided.

PERSONAL AND PROFESSIONAL RESPONSIBILITY

It is not enough for the members of an organization to refrain from harming others in the organization. They must display the same humane attitude the whole time so the standard of ethics is upheld in the organization. This should be thought of as achieving common good. And it is the duty of the HR leader to ensure the ethics of the organization. Along with individual rights, the diversity of cultures and people also must be protected. When an individual finds that she can assert her rights, she exercises similar care toward others who might depend on her for their well-being.

So, how does the HR manager instill her ethical belief in her employees? By becoming a better manager. She needs to cultivate a few characteristics that will aid her in her endeavor, becoming more self-aware, vigilant, perceptive, and considerate. Here are a few strategies for becoming a better manager:

1. Praise the Performers

Competent employees should never be ignored. Everyone wants acknowledgment and recognition. The fact that they do a good job does not mean that the HR leader can afford to ignore them. The HR professional must be careful not to give all her attention to her problem employees and unwittingly generate resentment among the rest of her staff. The employees who are fulfilling and—more often than not—exceeding the expectations also require attention. The HR leader must realize this and divide her positive and negative recognition accordingly.

2. Share Your Knowledge

Employees perform better when they are completely aware of the requirements of the job at hand. To enable employees to do their jobs effectively, the HR professional should clearly define the goals and objectives of the organization, the methods needed to improve, and every other strategy for success. When employees have an understanding of all these aspects, they will feel more vested in the company's success. In the process of communicating these details to employees, the style and manner of conversation of the HR leader also indicate that she considers the contributions and suggestions of her employees worthwhile, which makes them feel good and acts as a morale booster.

3. Schedule Meetings Only When Necessary

Meetings provide a wonderful opportunity to touch base and are a great platform from which to share concerns or ideas apart from being general get-togethers. But if meetings are held at every drop of a hat with no true concern for a topic, they merely waste everyone's time and energy. The HR professional, therefore, should take care that meetings get scheduled only when absolutely necessary. Additionally, if the HR leader is often seen in time-consuming management meetings, employees might well wonder if the department is really working. This can lower morale.

4. Engender Trust in Your Employees

Trust can be won only when the HR professional displays trust. When a competent employee proves herself worthy of the trust, the HR leader can bestow additional responsibilities on her. This will only happen as her confidence in the employee grows.

She should take care not to micromanage employees. She must not involve herself too directly with the employee's coordination of projects and solutions for problems, endangering relationships with clients. There is no point in damaging the business through micromanagement.

The HR manager, because of her unique position, has the responsibility to possess the vision and ideas that will drive the company toward its objectives. All the possibilities of the organization's human capital are at her disposal. She needs to communicate to her employees of the company's values and assure her employees that they will have a worthwhile stay in the organization. She should instill in them the desire to become part of the company's success.

Basically, the HR professional is required to be a leader. It has already been said that employees need to look up to somebody who embodies the organization. Who better than the HR professional? They expect to find values, commitment, and ethics that are inspiring enough to be followed, and they can successfully convey those on to customers after observing and internalizing them.

Raise the Bar, and Then Aim above It

When an individual becomes the HR manager of a company, that position of leadership requires her to be aware of company objectives and have confidence in its strategies and values. As leader, she should aim as high as possible. Her confidence will act as a source of inspiration for her employees, encouraging them to work beyond usual expectations. But goal-setting should not be unreasonable; the point should be set just above the attainable target to make the results satisfactory.

Cultivate Trust

As explained in chapter 4, the HR leader is the person who delivers, so she becomes the center of attention in the organization. She sets the example for how employees should conduct themselves and how the company identity should be communicated externally. Therefore, it becomes all the more important that HR be as transparent as possible, so everyone is in the loop about the company's direction. Straightforward and open communication signifies trust, and when employees realize HR's implicit trust in their potential, they will invest their best possible work to drive the company forward.

Identify Your Ideals, and Make Sure that Your Business Echoes Them

The HR leader is responsible for transforming ideas into realities. She must therefore have a clear vision and identity in mind for the organization. She must have a definition of work ethics and also have a clear notion of which values are important to her. She must understand which are the most and the least productive.

Then she should assess to what extent the company's ideals align with her. She must find out whether the existing practices of the company will enable her to incorporate her own ideals. The HR professional should adequately communicate to her employees that her core beliefs are vital to the organization. Her behavior must demonstrate her commitment to those values, only then is there a high probability of the company echoing this set of ideals.

Create a Culture of Collaboration

The HR leader is helpless without the support of her employees and the sustained satisfaction of the company's clients. Therefore, when she is chalking out her business strategies, she should consider both. She should communicate the objectives and aspirations of the company and invite employees to bring their suggestions and concerns. This is called "breeding collaboration" in the organization. In doing this, the HR manager is perceived as a leader who is sensible and sensitive enough to take everyone's ideas into account.

Employees become fond of a person who understands and takes care of their concerns. The HR leader cannot afford to rest at the stability of a situation. There is always the prospect of challenge when dealing with human capital. Lovable HR leaders must be equipped to deal with problems with alacrity and ease. When employees take liberties and stray from ideal work ethics, it affects the HR professional's decision-making and policy formulations.

It is the responsibility of the HR leader to design and enforce guidelines that ensure proper employee conduct and a productive workplace.

- The HR manager is responsible for documenting office policies, most frequently in the form of a handbook—issued at the start of employment—that has all the rules, regulations, procedures, and policies.
- Guidelines should be clearly set. There should be a clear distinction between performance deficiency and actual misconduct. Disciplinary measures should be strict so the company's core values are never in danger.
- The HR leader should keep her cool. She should be gentle but firm. Performance problems can be dealt with initially through training and counseling, but specific performance objectives and deadlines must be clarified in follow-up meetings until the issue is resolved.
- She should go with her guts. When in doubt, she should follow her intuition; it always tilts toward the right choice. In the case of performance deficiencies or increasing misconduct, the HR leader should take bold action, not letting problems slide and multiply.
- The HR manager must ensure fair treatment. She must make sure that every employee abides by the company guidelines, irrespective of position. Appreciation and motivation should be expressed as encouragement. The HR leader should express gratitude for great accomplishments.
- Before expecting loyalty from her employees, the HR leader should first be loyal to those employees' requirements and concerns. This will automatically generate positive results.

THE POLICY MANUAL

Management styles can be people- or product-oriented. An effective HR leader knows when and how to use which appropriate management style. She should be able to think out of the box and take the advice of policy managers in shaping the right management style. The selection of a particular management style depends on employee skills and knowledge, the available resources of time and money, and the desired results and particular problem or issue that the HR leader faces. This is important because, unless proper care is taken to select the specific style, the HR leader can well head down a slide of costly mistakes. A lovable HR is well-versed in company ethics and employee expectations and thus has the option of adhering to the style that perfectly fits to the given situation.

1. Participatory Style

Each employee can be given an entire task to complete. Or, if the employee is a part of a team for a particular project, the HR professional must ensure she understands her task completely. When the employee knows exactly where she fits in, she is more likely to feel motivated to complete the task. Apart from giving employees a sense of value, HR should encourage them to take ownership of the project. The HR leader should provide motivation and rewards for accomplishments. She must let her employees know that she has faith in their efforts.

2. Directing Style

A situation calls for a direct style of management when a project involves numerous employees or there is a tight deadline. The HR professional should answer five employee queries precisely: What? Where? When? Why? How? They will know what to do, how to get it done, and when they need to finish it. This style may seem cold and impersonal, but the HR professional can remain a motivating and accessible manager. She must still recognize and reward successes. Her manner of assigning roles and responsibilities, offering helpful direction, and sharing her experiences will increase her lovability quotient.

3. Teamwork Style

To expedite a project and optimize available resources, teamwork management is the best choice. When employees are motivated to pool their knowledge, the results can exceed all expectations. Well-coordinated efforts and sound and effective communication skills ensure successful teamwork. Clear and concise presentation of information leaves nothing unanswered, and when the HR leader genuinely credits the team for its success and independence instead of her savvy management skills, there can be no more creditable act in the eyes of her employees. The result is superior productivity, and the HR leader is loved even more!

.

Chapter 10

HR and the CEO: Always a Happy Couple

Avoid Clashes between Policy-Makers and Policy Enforcers

Being a great visionary or an exceptionally talented person is not enough without the support of an organization to help someone market her genius in the corporate society. Talent and support complement each other and achieve success.

In this case, the CEO and the HR manager of any organization need each other. With the combination of their individual talents, they can improve the work environment for the entire organization and all its employees. Together, they can sort out the challenges and the problems and build the company's future in perfect alignment with company objectives and work ethics. Working together has wider social implications, too. Well-coordinated action helps to build not only the company's future but also the associated families, the communities, and the world in its larger context. Undoubtedly, the HR manager is a profound force to reckon with.

HR deals with human capital, but before the HR leader can test her management skills with her employees, she has to establish a fundamental rapport with the organization's senior management—most importantly, the CEO. She needs to work in tandem with the CEO through a combination of drive, fortitude, and exceptional hard work. In the process, the HR manager has more opportunities to develop her skills as a leader.

Here are a few management techniques that the HR leader must follow to ensure effectiveness in her attempts to succeed:

She Should Get Advice from Top Management

The HR manager should establish a working professional relationship with senior management. It would be easier to do so if the business leaders earned their positions through their abilities. The HR leader would then find it easy to respect their judgment and discuss matters of concern with them. She should ask for their honest advice about what they think is essential for the overall growth of the company. Even if the HR manager thinks her CEO is not qualified or experienced enough to give an opinion on such matters, it will only add to her credibility and effectiveness if she is able to personalize communication with the CEO. The chance is high that the CEO will be flattered when asked for her opinion and be more than eager to bestow words of wisdom. This will help the HR leader establish a healthy relationship with the organization's management in the long run.

The HR Manager Needs to Step Up and Get Involved

The HR leader must always work to raise her visibility within the organization. The best possible way to do this is to expand her horizons and step beyond the limitations of her department to get involved in projects that involve a lot of other departments. This enhances her exposure, and she can reap the advantages of identifying with other members of the organization. She may also flex her leadership muscles in an appropriate way, depending on the situation, which will earn her bonus points with senior management. But she must make sure that her interest in the project is authentic and will enable her to be visible; appreciation is a secondary benefit.

The HR Leader Should Develop Her Credibility

People always like to work with individuals they trust and respect. So, the HR manager needs to build her credibility factor with senior management. To achieve this, she needs to build a healthy and trusting relationship with the CEO, which should be based on a *combination* of professional and personal factors working in tandem. This relationship can be achieved through effective and clear communication with the CEO. She should allow the CEO to speak and listen carefully and respectfully, regardless of the situation. If she makes any promises, she should keep her word. In case keeping a promise becomes impossible, she should explain the reasons and implications, offering any necessary fixes.

The HR leader should always keep in mind that she must never play favorites with any group in the organization; it always has a negative impact on her credibility. Similarly, she should avoid taking sides. It is always easier to influence a person if the other person respects her, so it should be a priority for the HR leader to earn that respect from her CEO and other senior business leaders.

The HR Manager Should Remember Her Subordinates
Though this section deals with the HR manager's relationship with her CEO, her relations to her subordinates are equally important. The manner in which the HR leader deals with her subordinates is a testament to her management and leadership skills for the CEO. The CEO identifies and nurtures the latent capabilities of the HR manager if she finds her able to help those working under her authority.

Everyone has a desire to grow, which is an important factor that, as a leader, the HR professional is able to encourage and motivate. The CEO will notice that the goals the HR leader has set for herself and her team are more likely to be accomplished in such a situation, because it adds to the cooperation and coordination of the HR manager and her team.

The HR Manager Should Speak Up
An effective leader is always associated with an inherent charisma, although—with proper learning—charisma can also be acquired. The HR leader should develop her social and public speaking skills, by volunteering to speak in service clubs and civic organizations. An effective speaker emerges only with the confidence of practice. The HR department demands such confidence. When dealing with human capital, it does not help to leave talent buried: people listen with care to, and get motivated and convinced by, a great speaker.

She Should Seek Variety
When one stays within the strict confines of a single unit, as said earlier, she is not only deprived of exposure but also faces monotony in her own work. As the saying goes, "Variety is the spice of life." Likewise, the HR leader should try her hand at different assignments, projects, and development processes. This will enhance her flexibility and help her think out of the box. Her innovative nature would gain ground,

and she could utilize her confidence to devise newer and more effective strategies for her employees and department. She will even feel like stepping away from the conventional path to find new challenges. As such, variety would enable the HR manager to add to the success of her team and the organization as a whole.

All of the above factors, when implemented in unison, remove the possibility of clashes between the policy-makers and the policy-enforcers. Senior management and the CEO are the policy-makers of the organization, and the HR leader is trusted to implement and apply those policies effectively and smoothly. A good understanding and healthy professional relationship with the CEO invariably helps the HR manager accomplish her goals more effectively.

But the interesting question is, "Will the HR manager and the CEO always be a happy couple?" A happy couple always makes a marriage work. They face challenges with combined effort, and their unity helps them emerge victorious. Disagreements can always arise, but there is no issue that cannot be resolved through effective communication.

The words *yes* and *no* have the potential to have great impact on endangering or endearing relationship. These simple words carry grave importance. They are so powerful that one must use caution in their proper application. Some instances in which *no* is the most appropriate answer in dealing with the CEO follow:

- "No, this critical fact needs to be documented because the employees already know it."
- "No, the situation does not require such an amount of nonsense because the employees are acquainted with the reality."
- "No, that new policy should not be imposed without a consultation session with employees."

The list can be added to infinitely. Undoubtedly, the CEO makes the decisions, but HR professionals implement them in the field. Therefore, they have a better understanding of employee mood and the possible outcome of a particular company policy. In situations in which there is a disagreement with the CEO, the HR leader should convince the CEO of her perspective by providing valid counterarguments. For an individual with some amount of genuine common sense, it is not at all a difficult task.

The point is, the HR leader should know where to draw the line. She is entrusted with an essential responsibility to improve the productivity of the organization, and she must guarantee that outcome. That is the basis of the integrity of the HR manager

But it is not only the *no* that is of great importance. A worthwhile *yes* is equally effective. Otherwise, the CEO might well come to believe that the HR department is nothing more than a bureaucratic obstacle to communication and implementation. She might think that the HR leader is holding her to an unachievable standard. The HR manager stands the risk of being perceived as unable to comprehend the business objective or true culture of the company, but that does not mean that the HR leader will settle for a *yes* with the CEO in such inappropriate occasions as:

- "Yes, that insanely cold and jargon-filled message will be published for all employees."
- "Yes, it is unimportant that you did not consult me before making that stupid decision."
- "Yes, whatever you say will be followed in exactly the same manner, and I do not mind being told what to do."
- "Yes, we can safely ignore these lousy employee survey results."

Those examples are probably enough to give one a clear idea of the meaning and the necessity of effective communication. It is important to understand the extent to which the HR manager can approach her job without compromising her integrity, the extent to which she can solve the organization's problems, and the extent to which she can earn that all-important trust, confidence, and respect from employees and the CEO alike.

To make a happy couple, the HR leader should become an executive coach for the CEO. The current group of company CEOs are mostly overworked and stressed out. They are naturally concerned about different work-life issues and time management. Therefore, the HR manager has emerged as someone who can enhance the satisfaction level of the CEO and help her find more balance in her life. What furthers this relationship is the effectiveness of leadership, communication, and team-building abilities of the HR leader. Thus, the relationship reduces the job stress of the CEO.

Apart from this, what the CEO looks for in her relationship with the HR manager is the psychological and political arenas at work. Both are intimately related to the HR leader's job requirements, and, if those aspects are not well-managed, job performance dramatically decreases. The CEO looks forward to establishing a relationship based in confidentiality, which she prefers to maintain in her direct and personal communication. The HR manager must aid her in her attempt and effectively maintain confidentiality.

The relationship is furthered through a servant leader orientation. The HR leader ought to possess a personality that can withstand and match the CEO's personality and demeanor. Furthermore, the HR manager should be equipped with experience, insight, and style. Clashes in style, behavior, and attitude are best avoided or there is the dangerous chance of the marriage breaking down.

The accurate understanding of each other's concerns and responsibilities make the union successful and can even revive a broken marriage. Life gets confusing when either the CEO or the HR manager underestimates the importance of plans for managing communications and retaining key talents. Without these plans, productivity is likely to slip, and the union is doomed to fail. It is all a matter of objective guidance and diligence. If the union dives toward doom in spite of all efforts, the HR manager must see the signals of when to quit, which begin when expectations envisioned prove unlikely to be carried forward. The HR leader probably needs to consider quitting when:

- the importance of HR as a discipline and the value of the function's intangible assets—measuring and improving human capital—fail to earn recognition or support.
- the CEO feels that winning the war either for talent or for customers must be the focus without seeing the need to balance these important priorities.
- the HR leader fails to receive support for her business strategies and operations. An experienced and competent HR manager need not suffer such humiliation

All of the above points relate the inefficiency of the CEO, but there can be situations in which the HR manager finds herself unable to fulfill her obligations. As a character of integrity, she should consider quitting when:

- she realizes that dealing with human emotions it not her forte. HR is all about loving the profession, and the job market is always hot for good professionals.

- the customer perception of the company is poor. Good perception requires effective communication and successful dealings.
- the inability to create an ideal work environment will inevitably affect productivity levels. There cannot be a worse situation than when the HR leader fails to acknowledge employee dissatisfaction or fails to improve employee satisfaction.
- the HR manager fails miserably as a decision-maker. She does not understand organizational dynamics or distinguish between politicking and positive political skills.
- the HR leader constantly finds herself building heroes out of senior management and the CEO and, in the process, persistently ignoring competent employees.

CONCLUSION

It is the caring and effective HR manager who ensures the success of any organization. A sensible HR manager is the fundamental requirement for this purpose. Only an individual possessing these qualities can demonstrate positive results.

The tide has always been in favor of the competent HR manager. She is the keystone of success. She seldom comes to the forefront to claim her success and receive due credit. After all, it is a noble profession. When loved by the team and the organization equally, and when the HR manager feels passionate about her job, there is no hurdle in her road to success. By right of her own accomplishments and abilities, she will no longer be merely a hatchet woman of the CEO.

She is destiny's child.

That is why I love HR.

www.ingramcontent.com/pod-product-compliance
Lightning Source LLC
Chambersburg PA
CBHW022018170526
45157CB00003B/1280